Prompted

AN INTERNATIONAL COLLECTION OF POEMS

Written by The Anthologists

With a foreword by Robert Lee Brewer

Edited by Dr. Pearl Ketover Prilik

RLYB

Prompted, an International Collection Of Poems

First Edition published 2011
by ReallyLoveYourBook
Unit 11, Concord House, Main Avenue, Bridgend, UK. CF31 2AG
www.reallyloveyourbook.com

ISBN   978-1-907375-94-1

Edited by Dr. Pearl Ketover Prilik
Cover photograph © 2011 Janet Rice Carnahan
Cover design © 2011 Michelle Hed

British Library Cataloguing in Publication Data.
A catalogue record for this book is available from the British Library.

Printed in the UK by Lightning Source, Milton Keynes.

Dedicated to Robert Lee Brewer
Without whom there would be no Poetic
Asides

FOREWORD
By Robert Lee Brewer

Sometimes, you get lucky. That's how I feel about starting the Poetic Asides blog. I still remember the meeting in which I proposed a poetry blog, a subject that had long been neglected by Writer's Digest. As a poet myself, I felt that somebody needed to make poetry a bigger part of the WD community. After a little back and forth, Poetic Asides was born.

The blog wasn't exactly focused in the beginning. The goal was to get at least two blog posts up each week (one by myself and one by former Poet's Market editor Nancy Breen) and that the posts had to have something to do with poetry. Eventually, I started covering poetic forms and interviewing poets. Then, I challenged poets to write a poem each day of April based off a daily prompt. To help with the process, I would share my own attempt at a poem too.

On the evening before the first-ever prompt, I remember telling my future wife—the poet Tammy Foster Brewer—I wasn't sure how many people would participate. Up to that point, we had a lot of page views, though not many comments. I was seriously expecting five or fewer poems each day—if that. Instead, there were more than 100 poems posted. And the rest is history.

The success of the first April challenge inspired me to post a weekly prompt (on Wednesdays) and create a November poem-a-day chapbook challenge. However, something more significant than just page views, poems, and comments started on April 1, 2008: A community was born.

Over the years, I've had the pleasure of watching the Poetic Asides community grow and shift and accomplish some truly amazing things—both as individuals and as a group. *Prompted* is one of those truly incredible group accomplishments.

When I look over the table of contents, I see poets who are spread around the country—and even the planet—who all share a love of poetry. I also see a group of connected voices who share their enjoyment in each other throughout the year. Often, I'm given a lot of credit for the strength of the Poetic Asides community, but I honestly feel like I was blessed with an amazing group of people. As this collection shows, I'm just one link in the chain; the poets who work well by themselves but also as part of a group make truly remarkable things come to life.

Prompted is filled with incredible poems by amazing poets. As usual, I feel lucky just to be invited to come along for the ride. Thank you!

INTRODUCTION
By Pearl Ketover Prilik & mike Maher. *

mike Maher.:

The idea for *Prompted* is something I floated earlier this year on the Facebook group page "PA Friends," which sprouted from the Poetic Asides community overseen by Robert Lee Brewer at Writer's Digest. At that time, it was just an idea, a seemingly insignificant passing thought which excited me enough to post it on the group page. I was sure nothing would come of it.

Not only did the community receive the idea warmly, but it quickly grew legs and began running. Heck, I think I even saw it on a unicycle navigating a trapeze wire. In fact, the idea for an anthology featuring the wonderful poets at Poetic Asides grew at such an exponential pace that it soon required its own Facebook group, one separate from the Poetic Asides page, just to keep track of its progress.

I should not receive, nor do I deserve, any credit for *Prompted*. All I did was put a few words down at Facebook and watch other people make them come to life. This book is a representation of the community at Poetic Asides - a group of loving, supportive people who believe in creation for the sake of creation, and that poetry in any form improves our daily lives.

Poetic Asides is the place where the poets featured in this anthology go to sing, bring news, and open their hearts to the opened hearts of others. Reading poetry is an integral part of writing poetry, and Poetic Asides is where we go to do both. Now, *Prompted* gives us the opportunity to share some of those poems with you.

* *mike Maher. is the poet's preferred spelling of his name.*

Pearl Ketover Prilik:

I agree with all mike Maher. has written. Whereas mike has a wonderful ability to get right to the heart of the matter, I often take a more strolling approach. I believe that this anthology is absolutely all that mike has suggested in his introduction. I also believe that *Prompted* illustrates both the collective spirit of poets and poetry and the power of the Internet, which is a fantastic force. Although in-person readings, and held-in-the-hand anthologies are thrilling, the power and sheer magnitude of connecting through online communities such as ours is stunning.

When I began submitting poetry online, I thought that this would be a limited pastime. If someone had predicted that a singular act would lead to three years of daily poetry writing and submitting I would have found it curious. If I had peeked through some psychic window into the future and seen a powerful group of diverse, internationally located, passionate poets connected one to another in a supportive community, linked by their love of the poetic word, I might have remarked, as Alice in Wonderland, "Curiouser and curiouser."

Through Robert Lee's Brewer's blog, I found the compatriots who appear in the following pages. Poetic Asides became, and continues to be, profoundly more than an "aside." This anthology is a product of some of the legions of poets who have responded to the daily prompts of April Poetry Challenges, November Chapbook Challenges, and/or weekly Wednesday prompts that usually run with ongoing commentary throughout the week.

I tried to ascertain the "it" factor that not only had Poetic Asides selected as a "blog of the year," but created a powerful sense of connection among poets. Was it Robert Brewer and his gift for prompts, the poetry, or his personality that played a huge role in the successful development of the community that arose and felt far more real than virtual? Certainly all of these traits, along with interviews, oversight when necessary, and the sharing of profound personal journeys and obvious enjoyment of his family all came together resulting in a rich environment of creativity and connectedness.

There was another essence at play here. Poets may be prompted by a multitude of stimuli from a flutter of the heart at a remembered love, the sparkle of water on the sea, an activists' need to bring about social change, or simply the inclination to sing one's song. When poets write together to a single prompt, everything from the magical or majestic can occur. When poets find a safe, supportive place to be heard, there is the possibility of transcendence. For a time, our group found themselves walking what came to be known to them as "The Street" and there found glimpses of the magical, the majestic and even the transcendent.

Being a part of this remarkable ongoing journey was not a personal isolated free fall. It was the sense of community born from this kaleidoscopic experience that had a group of international poets returning, many each day going beyond the poem-a-day challenges. Perhaps it is in this ability for poets to continue to write without distraction and yet simultaneously feel connected that is the true wonder that is expressed here through the work in *Prompted*.

Writing is in large part a solitary activity. The ongoing environment of living inside one's own head, accompanied only by a shadowy sense of motivation that either keeps words flowing or brings them to a halt can lend itself to a chilling loneliness. There are conferences and seminars and retreats, but perhaps the power of our supportive online community provided a unique opportunity to continue to write in solitude while in the "company" of others.

Poets are prompted by stimuli as individual as the poets themselves and yet perhaps this sense of connection provided by a group of "virtual" simultaneous creators collectively calmed this sense of occupational loneliness while empowering each other's individual voices. The sheer number of poems generated, shared, and the many publications springing from the site, throughout the years would give credence to this premise; although, of course, reasonable minds might disagree. However, it is unlikely that any would disagree that the ongoing sense of community has been the impetus for this collection.

The poets that contributed to *Prompted* are well known through their work and to one another. Many have been published previously online and in print, spanning the United States and Canada extending across the sea to Wales, Spain, and Germany.

Prompted is organized around 10 prompts that appeared over the years on Poetic Asides. We now share them, and ourselves, with you.

With special thanks to Writer's Digest for granting permission to include the chosen prompts; to Shannon Bo Lockard, who had an idea to create a Facebook group; to mike Maher. who "floated" an idea for a collection, was a participating poet, a terrific introduction writer, and a most welcomed eleventh hour once-over second pair of eyes; to the technical proficiency and enthusiasm of Paula Wanken, who custom-designed online surveys, posted reminders and assistance to move the anthology along, and created a poem to illustrate the sensibility of a prompt; to Michele and Andrew Brenton, our in-house publishers;, to Janet Rice Carnahan, for her illuminative cover photo; which represents the inspirational feel of poetry itself, and to the Michelle Hed's prowess in cover design. Thanks to the editor of Poetic Asides, Robert Lee Brewer, who never missed a single Wednesday prompt, November or April Challenge; and finally, a deep bow to the group of poets who call themselves The Anthologists, who decided to link across the expanse of the globe and leap into this anthology together, simply because we were all prompted to do so by the inexplicable force that moves us all to write and to share. It is our hope that you enjoy the poems and look for us again.

~ Dr. Pearl Ketover Prilik

Dear Poet:
I am new today.
You know I'm out here.
You know where to find me.
You know I will taunt and tease
until your muse comes looking for me.
And then your mind becomes not your own.
I take over, filling your thoughts with my words.
And my words will become your words which,
in turn, bring glorious new life to mine.
Together we'll create something.
I will be acknowledged, but
it is your name that will
be recognized as
the poet.

Sincerely,
The Prompt

"A Poet's Tease," was written for this anthology by Paula Wanken.

A Strand Poem* by "The Anthologists"
Written to the prompt "What prompts you to write?"

An infant eyelash on a newborn cheek , cinders of people dust and
all between (pkp)
She is prompted by the promise of phrases flung into the wind and
the prospect of watching them fly. (dj)

I write to hush the longings in my soul. (sb)
Poetry is love pouring out of my heart in metaphors and images
giving life to spiritual afflatus. (lk)

A creative welling up occurs within my being brought on by a scrim
of flowing silk, bit of red ribbon, speckled stone, cobalt colored
marble, fragment of pale aqua sea glass, bounce of wind in the end
of a pine bough, joy sparkling in one's eye; language of love,
surging in my blood, settling in my bones; overflowing in my spirit
and causing a hunger, a need to respond. (hg)

A skein, a web, a snarl of words gently untwists and becomes
something beautiful. (dtc) words become pictures and pictures
become poems. (pw)
Emptying out my brain's contents, one poem at a time. (jh)

Here are some words; here is a road. Create your journey. (bn)
From prompt to pen to page, an unbroken path of poetry or prose--
it's all good! (ch)

Words rush from my fingers when the spark of my muse is ignited.
(be)
A persistent itch at the back of my brain. (mb)

If you can say everything you need to say in just 17 syllables - and
make people laugh in the process - you are a true success. (rjc)

The sands of time are just made of sand but the water of life
touches every soul (idk)
The loves of my life -- all the laughter and cries (ab)

A sight or sound, taste or smell, feeling or thought; in everything
and anything, my muse can be found. (lh)
Nature captured by my eye, makes my pen move. (mh)

Gossamer strands of understanding stick until I weave them into
what they were meant to feel. (pah)
writing like breathing, breathing for living (ak)

morning walk beneath blue sky, whirr of dragonfly, scent beyond
my eye (jph)
a click and a spark that will push this rolling stone, which moves a
bit faster with moss overgrown. (amt)
Bobbing in a sea of too much to do when I found you (sv)
and the tongue is a mighty and delicate muscle when it moves the
pen or takes the wheel (da)
It begins as a whispered vision until it glistens in the sun of reality.
(jrc)
I bend with ink-stained hands to gather words beneath the surface.
(cl)

A whisperer electrifies my brain (cjy)
I am not an artist. I am a documentarian and I am my own favorite
subject. (bm)

The focus to find a little piece of peace in pinning down that bit of
something that is Me. (nm)
This world is a lost jungle, just longing for us to paint its walls with
carefully inked leaves. (kh)

Sometimes at night, I waken, not from the sound of a rattle of
someone trying the door or tree branches tapping against the
window or soft footfalls outside my door, but the muse, whispering
lines in my ear, prodding me to reach for a pen and paper, to
capture them before they too slip back outside. (np)

Sometimes out of the darkness of the soul; sometimes, skimmed
from the lightest part of everything – words to hammer and twist
and weave until they make sense or don't – poetry saves me, is the
best and the worst of me. (sei)

Sculpting beauty with words, as the world was beautifully formed
by the great Creator's words. (ej)
With pen in hand I'll take a stand and sing of love from up above."
(mg)

I like wrapping my feelings into little word packages, so when
others open them, they laugh, cry, and experience life. (cp)
the desire to get out some of what has gotten in, to drain the
overwhelming basin of being, to live a little longer through every
word on paper. (mm)

words pour from wounds that eyes can't see, a blood soaking into
pages, like a poultice drawing out a poison from the broken heart
of beauty unseen. (jz)

If the jaundiced sun punches a hole in the parchment sky, I must pen those words or expire. (kk) a smile, a tear, a stifling fear (sbl)

Writing requires at least as much attention as a person would devote to a friendship. If I ignore them for too long, words won't come when I call them. Due diligence and faithfulness to my own truth keep me observing, writing, and monitoring the undercurrents of my life where real discovery is made possible. (js) Wherever my mind wanders, my best chance is to catch up with it (abl)

* A "Strand" poem is a coined term for a collective poem of combined lines written by a group of individual poets and "strung" together without editing to form a naturally flowing poem.

THE PROMPTS, THE POETS & THE POEMS

A list of prompts as they originally appeared on the blog Poetic Asides may be found in the Appendix at the conclusion of this book.

If the jaundiced sun punches a hole in the parchment sky, I must pen those words or expire. (kk) a smile, a tear, a stifling fear (sbl)

Writing requires at least as much attention as a person would devote to a friendship. If I ignore them for too long, words won't come when I call them. Due diligence and faithfulness to my own truth keep me observing, writing, and monitoring the undercurrents of my life where real discovery is made possible. (js) Wherever my mind wanders, my best chance is to catch up with it (abl)

* A "Strand" poem is a coined term for a collective poem of combined lines written by a group of individual poets and "strung" together without editing to form a naturally flowing poem.

THE PROMPTS, THE POETS & THE POEMS
A list of prompts as they originally appeared on the blog Poetic Asides may be found in the Appendix at the conclusion of this book.

PROMPT 4 - PRAYER

PROMPT 5 - LOVE/ANTI-LOVE POEM

PROMPT 6 - TYPE OF PERSON

PROMPT 9 - ALL I WANT

PROMPT 10 - AFTER LEAVING HERE

Prompt 1

TIME OF DAY

Beer Thirty
Nikki Markle

Steeled toed boots
Kicked off by the door
Pepper the
Floor with flakes of
Mud. Worn jeans,
Once-white socks, a

Flannel shirt with loose
Buttons leave a
Trail like
Breadcrumbs to the
Chair where a callused
Hand pulls the
Tab and marks the
End of the work day.

Mid-Day Crisis
Jay Sizemore

When the sun reaches its apex,
it starts to panic
about its remaining six hours
on this side of the Earth.
It wonders how many
of the girls down below
blow kisses at the moon
while he is away.
He grows self-conscious
of the growing number
of solar flares on his girth,
wonders if he is still as hot
as he was when the planets
were just being born.
He wishes for hands and ears
to adorn with jewelry,
wishes he was cool enough
to not turn all metal into vapor
so he could own a new Corvette.
His mind races with "what if's,"
what if the world changes while he's gone,
what if his light isn't enough,
what if he doesn't rise again?
He thinks about the past,
about the girl in the white dress
who hides in the moon
on the other side of the world,
wonders if she's happy,
dreams of their next eclipse,
and what he might say
to make her smile
if he gets another chance.
The hours wane
as he sidesteps the horizon
in their timeless waltz,
relinquishing his light for
her softer spell,
catching just a hint
of her powdered perfume.
Each time he knows
it could be the last,
his nuclear reactor heart
was never meant
to be unbreakable.

12:34 p.m.
Janet Rice Carnahan

A time that doesn't come around,
All that often,
Oh, wait a minute,
I guess maybe it does.
And when it does,
I have an agreement,
With a fabulous male friend,
That we will send each other,
A positive thought,
Each time,
Every time,
It shows up on our clock.
We just liked the way,
It all lined up,
And made sense,
To us,
Like our relationship did,
Each time,
We could make time for,
Each other!

A long time ago,
We had such a connection.

Maybe it's about time I say hello.
Yes, maybe it's just about . . .

Time!

8:46...9:03...10:03
Paula Wanken

a sunny morning
nothing out of the ordinary
running late for work

putting on makeup
doing my hair
listening to the Today Show

the exact time is unknown
I didn't look at the clock
but time was about to stand still

8:46
9:03
10:03

those aren't the numbers I remember
the ones that stick in my head are
9 and 11

3:03 p.m.
Salvatore Buttaci

three became my lucky number
after years and years of being let down
by five and seven and thirteen

three that I never gave a thought about
became that afternoon suddenly magical
because you stood beside me

three of us—you and I and Father Ed--
and behind us three times twenty
oohing and aahing as we exchanged vows

three took on new meaning
as we said the binding "I do"
and walked as one out of St. Stan's

3:03 p.m. I know because in my nervousness
I glanced down at my watch
like a man late for an appointment

three of us till the last clock ticks--
you and I and our God
Whom we follow one step at a time

4:11 P.M.
S.E. Ingraham

Wednesday, an ordinary middle-of-the-week
Hump day, late afternoon, run-of-the-mill
Nothing happening type time really

But then, the big-hand on the wall clock
of the hospital's open-air eating area
clicks from the ten to the eleven

And my no-nonsense steps,
The brisk walk of a person eager
To depart the hospital is halted
Pretty much mid-stride

My senses, my aural senses
Are assaulted by a symphony
Of sound, so authentic, so rich and fine

I begin searching the enormous space
That makes up this open concept
Hospital for the philharmonic

Convinced I will see them
Seated on one of the four
Visible levels

I do not
But the music plays on;

I finally grab a chair at the nearest table
As much under the "sweet" spot
As possible – casting around wildly

Is it just me?
No—I begin to notice others
Stopping, searching, smiling, bemusedly...

Oh, now, this tears it—
A pause in the playing
And there is applause
And cheers of "Bravo"

Where are they, I wonder?

Then, as they strike up
Beethoven's Pathetique
And I am lost in the music ...

Does it really matter?
Do I need to see them to
Enjoy this?
Perhaps not...

Three O'Clock P.M., October 26, 1881
Diana Terrill Clark (Domino)

The real facts may never be known
because, as they say,
history is written by the victors
and the victors were definitely
the Earps.

Thirty shots were fired
in as many seconds;
two fled, three dead,
and of course, the victors were
the Earps.

And though the facts are
sharply contested to this day,
the most famous gunfight of all time,
at the Okay Corral, the victors were
the Earps.

7:44
Connie Peters

The porch bell sits silent—at last.
I took it down to stop its clanging.
The wind rustles the bushes
with barely discernible buds,
promising spring,
but the slate gray sky
threatens snow.

A single truck roars by,
announcing morning.
Most of the neighborhood argues—
it's still night since it's Saturday.
I hear groans and shuffles back the hallway.
My family agrees with the truck.
Time to get breakfast.

Night Rising
Hannah Gosselin

Hushed rushing
of dark waves
upon sandy shore.
Hollow echo,
water filling
cavernous tidal pools.
Wind pressing forth
against silhouetted tree-tops.
Frogs find their voice
lifting them on the breeze.
Crickets add fiddle
to the melodic song.
Collective serenade.
Moon's arrival;
simple, pure elegance.

B.C
Elizabeth Johnson

Two bubbles of baby blue look out
under eyelids still heavy with sleep,
blankly staring at the long day
looming ahead, the bleakness
of never ending to do lists, the
curse of too few hours in the day.

They wrestle half-heartedly with
eyelids that want to sleep, drawn
by the sunlight peeking around
bedroom curtains but lulled to
sedation by larger darkness. Slowly
they open wholly and make way

down the hall, past the sleeping
dog, past clocks announcing the time,
past animated neon lights, into the
haven, where those baby blues light
upon stainless steel and glass, half
full already with steaming black gold,

that brew of champions, nectar of
liquid perfection, which calmingly
arouses the senses and wakens them
to the optimism of a new day. Somehow
the world seems less bleak after a few
sips of sweet creamy breakfast blend.

*B.C. - before coffee

Eleven Eleven
Michael Grove

Those who study numbers have a premise.
Linked perhaps by chance or coincidence,
are events that take place only at these times.
Synchronicity the fiddler at this dance.

Others say the sign is quite auspicious
More believe the spirits' presence here.
New age philosophers say "mystic powers"
Post-hoc reasoning, the skeptics fear.

But those alive who truly see this window,
With those who were once here, but whom have passed.
Communicate directly thru this portal.
Ripples this still pond. The stone is cast.

The Back Room Of McGinty's
Amy Barlow Liberatore

There's a bar in Hell's Kitchen
West of the West Side
Smells of cabbage and Guinness and hard-earned sweat
Front room's for hard drinkers watching a rabbit-eared TV

But come with me on a Monday evening
to the back room of McGinty's
lit by one weak bulb strung off the ceiling
like a hangman's noose

Tables crammed with some-lately IRA men
surrounded by long-since immigrants

One strapping singer stands, hat in his hands
to offer "Four Fields"
His tremulous tenor rings, bringing forth tears
through smiles of remembrance

Another robust in his delivery
gives us "I Don't Want To Join The Army,"
and when the lines come true,
"I don't want a bullet in me backside,
I don't want me buttocks (or arsehole) shot away,"
he blushes but the men all beat the tables and come-what-may

On and on the music flows
Even if you're never trod the Olde Sod
your heart is forever touched
sentimental and melodious
when your blood flows truly Irish

© 2010 Amy Barlow Liberatore

8:23 - 1970 - 1990
Pearl Ketover Prilik

It was the newest precision watch, accurate in unmatched accuracy
Correct to a fractional second promised no deviation ever would be

He was fascinated in one thousand, nineteen hundred and seventy
Called the time on the telephone regularly, smiling as he watched
the second hand click in perfect synchronicity

The best science of the day brought him this watch, this Accutron
Used by NASA to launch, yet, an alarm beeped each evening
although neither set nor turned on

In the beginning all searched for meaning as to what would 8:23
anticipate?
As any event drew near all would think perhaps this time could be
the date

Graduations, engagements, weddings, beginnings of each new
career
New lives were born, some others died, surgeries, accidents,
surprises, all sorts of events came quite near

Things happening at all sorts of times obviously
Yet, as the years melted one to the other nothing happened at 8:23

Except, of course for the alarm which part of him came not quite
awaited yet welcomed to be
Whether in a Land Rover in red dusted safari, or in the first row of
a Broadway musical show he did see

That single dignified beep blipped each evening at home or away
Accepted and smiled at, with nary a question nor any more there to
say

He never did fix it, never would hear of a potential repair
Perhaps there was a reason or not, he did not either way care

The beep was part of the precision at eight twenty and three
Every evening for twenty years a beep beeped faithfully

His quiet crisp immediately identified signature sign
A tiny town crier whispering he was near all was well, all was fine

Until a searing hot summer came with a definite medical end
And though no one said it all wondered if 8:23 was finally its
message to send

On that last day as he slept, woke and breathed in the air of
another atmosphere
All watched and all waited as the sun set and 8:23 moved nearer
and near

He died the next morning at 11:11 ... Not 8:23
Although it would have been pretty, death is not poetry

8:40
Nancy Posey

I love the exactitude of parents
of newborns—reporting the birth
in the tiniest increments—
labor began at 1:57. (Digital clocks
were invented and time grew more
precise.) She was born at 8:40,
weighing 8 lb., 4 oz., 21 ½ inches long
(as if anyone, trained or not, could
measure with certainty the springy
length of a baby child fresh
out of the womb, stretching, reaching
for boundaries no longer there).
They measure her age in days,
then weeks, then months, until
she is old enough to take over
the count: I'm two and a half.
I'm going on five. Perhaps numbers
are a comfort, something objective
to report, holding back the truth:
she is beautiful, so beautiful,
the most beautiful child ever born.
And she's ours.

6:52
Sara Vinas

Eyelids weighted
By dreams that wish
To tumble back
Into darkness
Resolved to ignore the breeze
Whispering frond windsongs
I drift and seek
My dreamship
"It's pink," he calls
Vision refocuses
From fantasy to reality
Eyelids flutter like the linen curtains
He's pulled aside
Stretching, I step onto tile
Chilled like morning sea sand
And tiptoe outside
The eastern sky gives me a rosy
Air brushed greeting
While the coconut palm fronds
Wave, then catch
The glowing orb
Like a high fly ball

Prompt 2

INVERTED PYRAMID

The Perfect Guglhupf
Cara Holman

The most important thing
is the flour and sugar.
Shortening and eggs
hold it all together.
A bit of leavening,
salt to taste,
the merest suggestion
of lemon peel.
Raisins, they're optional.
Mix it, stir it,
put it in a pan
and bake until done.
Dust with confectioner's sugar
and eat while still warm.

Capers for Dinner
Claudette J. Young

Robbery seems to have been the motive
For a break-in at the Hazard Inn this weekend.
Two dark-clad figures, wearing ski masks,
Found themselves dinner guests at the home of
Vlad and Elma Shivers of Betchado Point.
It's believed these weren't local fellows since
They were unaware that the Shivers don't
Use lights at the Inn. The result: the criminals
Entered the dining room to find sharp
Instruments and pointed smiles aimed at them from
The table set for a late dinner hour.
There is no report as to the current whereabouts
Of said criminals. It's believed they
Sought to explore other, less challenging pastimes.

Four-Year-Old Kaitlin Jones

Pearl Ketover Prilik

The body of four-year-old Kaitlin Jones found today
Mutilated, raped, and murdered in unknown order
Kaitlin had been missing for three weeks
Police had called in the FBI after an Amber Alert failed and no leads were uncovered
A search party had been organized by friends and family
Her mother screamed when night fell and Kaitlin was not found
It had been expected the strong-willed little girl was hiding
Kaitlin had been under the care of Dr. Goode, PhD and categorized as oppositional
defiant/conduct disordered
Her grandfather thought she was just a little girl who knew what
she did and did not want
But even he had to agree that something was wrong when Kaitlin was not found in
any her 'private' places where she often
stayed for hours on her own
The family was never under suspicion of any foul play
Neighbors responded to the mother's screams, coming together
in their nightclothes
Making coffee, flyers and organizing search parties, some brought their untrained
dogs on long leashes, others stayed with the family
keeping up a stream of platitudes
The day Kaitlin disappeared she had been given a peanut butter and jelly sandwich
with the crusts on and
the jelly rather than the peanut butter on top
Kaitlin had fallen to the floor shocking the new baby-sitter with her screams
A moment later she ran from the kitchen into her room and slammed the door
Kaitlin's room was on the ground floor
In case of such a 'melt-down' the baby-sitter had been instructed to let Kaitlin "be"
No one noticed four-year-old Kaitlin climb from her window and
drop to the ground
Where she ran across the field toward the wooded hiking trail that snaked into the
woods
Along the highway unseen but heard
rushing in the distance
beyond the trees
Where a young man had parked his car, walked for a while and
waited for something to happen –
Like a four-year-old girl who didn't like her peanut butter and jelly sandwich.

First Night
Andrew Kreider

The production of Oklahoma!
was a smash hit, drawing
five hundred eager spectators to the
outdoor stage on the Civic Plaza.
A cast of local residents having worked six months
to mount the show were gratified that the threatened
thunder storms held off until long after the final
applause had echoed from the drug store wall.

Audience members sweltered happily for three
hours, consuming large quantities of succulent
barbeque and anonymous white wine.
The girls on stage, meanwhile, twirled in
homespun pinafores, clacking character shoes
on rough wood while veering to avoid the
old man gamely supporting the wall of Jud's
smokehouse, flapping in the stiffening breeze.

There were no injuries and no emergencies,
only periodic sirens from the shiny fire trucks
high steppin' from the central station, brightly fringed
surreys with their sidelights blinking in the Indiana night

Prompt 3

MESSAGE IN A BOTTLE

Ars Poetica

Daniel Ari

One time I found a bottle on the shore.
Although the cork was eaten down by salt
and sand, the neck was still stoppered. The vault
inside held wine, a sea-seasoned liqueur.
When I lifted the blasted glass to look,
two tiny spiders dropped into the breeze,
parachuting from the height of my eyes
from the minute caverns of the half cork.
Brine wine sloshed opaque legs around the wall.
Amazed I raised the vintage in a toast:
to The Mystery. To this precious coast.
To surprises borne here by unknown squalls.
What's wondrous can't be worthless. Take the wine
and the sea and the seer and the rhyme.

Bottled Up

Jacqueline Hallenbeck

Place your woes into a bottle
and toss 'em in the ocean.
Be it obstacle or hurdle,
place your woes into a bottle,
picture yourself back in the saddle;
giving up is NOT an option.
Place your woes into a bottle
and toss 'em in the ocean.

Once Full
Paula Wanken

this bottle, once full,
serves as a reminder
of how empty my life is without you

your words, you used
to knead my wounded soul,
no longer echo in this world

your touch, you used
to melt away my fears,
is no longer felt in this world

your love, you gave
to cleanse my picture of self,
is no longer given in this world

this bottle, now filled with my words,
serves as a reminder
that my life can be full once more

To Whom It May Concern
Bruce Niedt

Don't bother looking for me.
I'm sure this island isn't on the map.
I've made a spear to snag
all the fish I can eat, and I've
developed a taste for coconut.
Dried banana leaves make
great writing paper, and
some little squid-like creature
has provided plenty of ink.
The vehicle for this missive
is courtesy of a washed-up
crate of Chianti, so I'll continue
to post via oceanic mail
from time to time, and write
as quickly as I can drain
the contents of the bottles,
brave little postmen who bob
on the tides and wash on your shore
to tell you I'll be fine,
at least until the last drop.

To Whom it May Concern
Catherine Lee

No one
Heard me today
Though I raised
The loudest clamor

I put on words
Thick as clown white
Black as teardrops
Under each eye

The world is large
It swallows me
In easy gulps
Like medicine

Empty
Kim King

The ink had dried, cursive letters swirled
over parchment-- frosting decorating a cake
without candles. He rolled the paper, a telescope,
aimed it at the sea, and then sealed it with red wax
that she had bought him in Florence. He smelled
the crema on the espresso and her Versace perfume,
always that perfume! Notes of citrus and jasmine
over sandalwood. He sniffed the paper.
It was still there, embedded in the fibers.
He took the empty bottle of Brunello and stuffed
the roll inside. Plunk, it hit the bottom, the green glass
thick and cold. He held the stained cork, squeezed,
turned, and used both hands to push it down.

Farewell Message
Connie Peters

Since you're reading this, I'm probably dead.
So to my hubby, I say from my heart,
though there were crumbs, we didn't trash the bread,
yet, the first thousand years, let's live apart!

If you, my dear daughter, first read this note,
I'm proud of the person you have become.
And to my sweet son who's smart, but remote,
I love you a lot, but don't be a bum.

If a friend or stranger happens to find
this short message among all of my socks,
take whatever you like or comes to mind
and put the rest in a give-a-way box.

On the other hand, I may still be here.
Thank you for doing the laundry, my dear.

Floater
Jane Shlensky

On deserted but
livable island
fresh water
lovely skies
occasional storms
tropical fruit and fish
modest hut
no mortgage
no job
no taxes
lots of time
to write on leaves
in sand.
Float me a line
some time

No Deposit, No Return
De Jackson

                     You
                     put
                     me
                     here
                at the bottom
                of this amber
                glass, beneath
                your lies and
                your broken
                smile. Drank
                it all, poured
                me down and
                tossed it into
                the vast ocean
                that has some
                how spilled be
                tween us like a
                shark infested
                moat. But see
                    here's the
                  thing: I float.

Tears
Elizabeth Johnson

You have kept count of my tossings; put my tears in your bottle.
Are they not in your book? Psalm 56:8

sorrows overwhelm
drown my eyes
break before you

griefs boil over
rise like the tide
overflow your bottle

remorse, regret
trickle away
baptize your book

Cast
Michael Grove

I'm sending you this message,
In a bottle so that we
may find each other someday
and our love will come to be.

So I write a little note now
As I cast it out to sea,
I will say a prayer of hope,
and wait here patiently.

I'll let the currents take you
to the place that you should be,
as I cast away my message
for awaiting destiny.

This sealed note is for anyone
riding on the ocean blue
for the words capped in this bottle,
Simply say that, "I Love You."

Message in Your Bottle

Shannon Bo Lockard

I should have placed a message in every
bottle you brought to your lips. Explaining
how space widened between us with each sip.
I would have written, "I love you. You are
worth more than a bottle of Schnapp's. I need
you. Please stop!" I do think of you from time
to time. Wonder how life is treating you
and whether you think of me, too. But, I've
learned to live without you. Pulled myself up,
your bottle forever sealed our fate.

Message in a Bottle

Amy Barlow Liberatore
(For my mother... rest in peace)

For the first time in years
(and so welcome, this occasion)
seated across the kitchen table with Mom.

For the first time in years
(since I headed west for a spell)
she was not drunk.

There was a message in
the absence of a gin bottle...
Gordon's had been her steadfast companion

Now we sat and looked each other in the eye
"Amy," she said kindly, "there's a scratch in your voice.
You need to stop smoking pot."

For the first time in years,
we spoke singer to singer, our voices had always been
our beauty, our careers, our all.

"I sobered up," she said slowly, "cold turkey."
It was true - too ashamed to go to a clinic,
knowing so many people in town.

Dad had gone to her door several times each day,
listening to the retching, passing in black coffee
and soda crackers for a solid two weeks.

But for me, quitting a joint a day was easy.
And so the message was clear: No more bottle for her,
no more buds in Buglers for me. Saved my life, she did.

© 2010 Amy Barlow Liberatore

41

If You're Still Alive
mike Maher.

This is not like the time in high school
when you wrote a letter to yourself
and your teacher mailed it to you five years later
and nothing was as you expected,
not even the parts you thought you could get out of.
It's not like that at all.

For a while they rolled out new versions of products
which were the same products
only now they beeped when they wanted attention.
Beeep, beeep, beeep, your microwave says,
the popcorn is still done.
Does everything beep in the future?

If you have managed to make it this far,
congrats on surprising me, amigo.
Are gnats an endangered species yet?
What about those green flies that bite you
when you're focusing on not stepping on the bottom of the lagoon?

Our problems must seem silly to you now,
especially once the polar ice caps melted
and underneath they found more polar ice caps,
no need to worry.
It's just like that picture you won on the cruise ship that time,
the wooden ship floating next to the aircraft carrier.

Your name was mike Maher.,
you carved your life story into a tree at Columcille,
right below the heart and the ribbons.

Alice's Adventure
Sara Vinas

Dear Alice
Impetuousness clearly
Runs strong in your family
Did your parents not
Teach you to stay
Away from strange bottles?
Or strange rabbits?
Or not to believe everything
You read?
Still it will be a grand adventure
Just remember what the caterpillar
Said
And keep your head

Prompt 4

PRAYER

relationship meditation
Daniel Ari

Yin yang separates into two beings:
the white-eyed black fish flies northeast and up
the black-eyed white bird swims southwest and down.
Individual experience is
so wondrous, each entity is lonely
for a counterpart with whom to share all.
They trade their eyes for a perfect partner,
go blind for an embrace that makes a whole.
They whirl in the ecstasy of union.
and when they find stillness, they separate.

Dear God... (Baby Faith's Prayer)
Jacqueline Hallenbeck

After mommy tucks me in...
...please keep an eye on her.
She loves me more than anything.
After mommy tucks me in,
turn her frown into a grin,
let her woe become a blur.
After mommy tucks me in...
...please keep an eye on her.

To Make Our Crown (A Child's Confession to Mother Earth)
Patricia A. Hawkenson

The daisies once
held dew in their cups,
enough to spare
as the caterpillars crawled up.

But our knees scratch
with the dust of drought,
our eyes unable
to cry enough tears.

For we had torn
the daisies up
and now the ground
will bare no more.

We are left to play
tic-tac-toe in the dust
with sticks and stones
our mocking jewels.

A Prayer for the Preantepenultimate
RJ Clarken

It's tough to be the fourth in line.
You're stuck in what seems bad design.
But lest you think you're much harassed,
thank God that you are fourth; not last.
Unless, they are both one and same.
That really would be quite a shame.
But even if that's what you find,
it's not a queue: it's state of mind.

If A God Should Be Listening
S.E.Ingraham

In between the lines of the music
And the breaths the choir staggers
As they sing each note, forming
A perfect, cohesive whole

Every time an icicle drips one flawless
Tear-shaped drop upon ground
Thirsting for springtime

When the laughter of children
Shatters the solemnity of tragic
Circumstances and lightens darkness

If a God should be listening, surely
He will approve and approving
Bless us with his benevolence

And in this way, we may all begin
To believe again ...

Looking Up
Laurie Kolp

You lift me up
hope and love
eternal life
with you above.
You cleanse me from consuming fears
I offer you trust, you wash away tears
Remove bad habits, empty evil desires,
With you, I'm whole- no peace expires.
My dearest God, I pray to you on high
Lead me forward, I'll reach the sky.
You lift me up
hope and love
eternal life
with you above.

Legacy Worth Remembering
Hannah Gosselin

Lord, I pray that one day my eyes will shine behind a face of full wrinkles written in laughter, love, sadness, dancing, wishing , living; scripted into my soul, my skin, my bones, by the seconds, minutes, days and years spent trying to live life according to Your will for me. Father, I pray that my life will exemplify an image of Your Son, just a spark of the unconditional love that we've been gifted. I pray that when my last breath's being drawn through wisdom, withered lips or smooth, young ones that I will hold no regrets and that I will have lived a legacy worth remembering. That I would look within and see less of me and more of You. I pray in the name of Your Precious Son. Amen.

Sunrise Service (Easter 2011)
Andrew Kreider

You lipsticked cigarette ends
circling smoke to heaven,
rampant weeds defying mulch
and axel-breaking potholes:
Praise the Lord.

You blissed-out muzak
Kenny G-ing overhead,
slick-haired TV talking heads
and day-old business pages:
Praise the Lord.

You pouting teenage girls
in long skirts and too much makeup,
freckled younger brothers
and disapproving grandmas:
Praise the Lord.

You harried first-generation immigrants
screwing up my order,
overflowing coffee pots
and abandoned egg mcmuffin:
Praise the Lord.

You white-clothed street crew
worn out from your heavy lifting,
you military veterans
stealing glances at the
women in the corner

by the empty table.

you military veterans
stealing glances at the
women in the corner

by the empty table.

God's Confessional
Catherine Lee

Your pain is familiar,
Like each silver scar across
My skin that you won't touch.
I am big enough to handle
The anger you hope
Will push me away.

This is not how the story ends.
The sun will rise to shake the days
And nights and all the hidden
In between spaces where you hide
Because redemption is a monster
To be afraid of.

So sit in cobwebs as you weep
While I watch tired feet
That run too long.
Then come and sit
With me a little while.
I sing words you do not know,
But I know them by heart.
You see, I wrote each letter
Red
For you.

Mustard Seed Prayer

Michael Grove

Please Dear Lord, come be our guest,
we give you thanks, as we are blessed,
with all your Grace and Glory be,
ours for all eternity.

We humbly bow our heads in prayer,
and sing our thanks that You are there,
for each of us in time of need,
and for the tiny mustard seed.

The faith we sing within our heart,
Raise us up with a youthful start.
Your kingdom which was once so small,
Is now the greatest of them all.

God's Courtroom
Elizabeth Johnson

I enter the court and the judge
stands before me, righteous and
demanding of the same from me,
who knows only wickedness.

I cower before him, wanting to hide
my weakness, my filth, ashamed
to even look at his face, in his eyes,
knowing my sentence too well.

I shudder to think of the years
that must be spent abandoned
in some dark place of torture,
left only with my own stench.

I hear then- more than a whisper,
like a gavel slamming down- the
pronouncement, my sentence;
someone must pay the price.

I wonder astonished when I hear
that my life has been pardoned!
my transgression wiped clean, that
I no longer live with my sentence.

I stand amazed in the presence
of my upright judge, who has paid
the price of my crime with his blood,
pardoned me through his own pain.

I look and he calls to me, longing
for friendship with me, wanting me
like a father estranged from his child,
yearning for me to come home.

I run to him, boldly approaching his
throne, eager to talk and to know him,
hearing his thoughts, sharing them,
trusting his offering of love for me.

A Mother's Prayer
Kim King

Children, breathe in the sunshine that ripens the blueberries,
gooseberries and rhubarb, your favorites. Please, protect
each other and your earth. Open the door and smell
the fresh-cut grass. Brush the lavender with your fingers
and taste a licorice leaf of tarragon. Pet dogs behind
the ears and hold your hand flat to give a sugar cube
to a horse. Pick up your socks and don't dust unless
you have company. Use cold, fresh water to make tea
and warm the ceramic pot. Wake up early to see the
sun rise over the trees and hear the woodpecker's staccato
drumming. Breakfast is the most important meal
of the day. It fuels you and lets your head wake up
while you prepare it. Remember to cherish each other.
You three will be left to carry on the family traditions.
Marry someone who will share and celebrate with you.
God bless you and keep you safe. Turn off the lights.

Prayer for Just Enough
Buddah Moskowitz

Lord,
please bring us world peace
but just enough to keep things
tranquil
without becoming boring.

Please bring us good health
but just enough
so that our own occasional
ache and pain
will remind us to have compassion
for others' hardships.

Bring us prosperity
but just enough
so that no one ever goes to bed
hungry
and that no one ever becomes
possessed
by their possessions.

Let us be sure
of your infinite forgiveness
but just enough
so that we never cheapen
your grace
by taking it
for granted.

Lord,
let us love one another
and take care of one another
just enough
to eventually
replace this list
of petitions
with an endless psalm
of thanksgiving.

Baruch Hashem Adonai.

Prayer From The Heart

Janet Rice Carnahan

May all souls everywhere,
Rejoice in the true beauty they are.
May they remember that beyond all,
Anger, despair, grieving, turmoil and sorrow,
There is Love and that Love is never ending.
When we surrender to that Love,
There is so much more clarity,
There is so much more Truth.
And may they know,
When we can surrender to that Love,
Our hearts can open, individually, collectively!
Our souls can connect, individually, collectively!
Back to that sense of ONENESS,
Which will always carry us forward . . .

In continual Love and Peace.

Prompt 5

LOVE-ANTI/LOVE POEM

Mortar & Pestle
Nikki Markle

Aerial acrobatics of winged spirits and
Wishful thinking swirl
Patchouli through the candlelight.

Scrape of stone on stone,
Round and round.

Rose petals for your heart,
Thyme is for commitment,
Clove, to open your eyes, and
Lilac for empowerment.
Willow, bluebell, and bay
Add power to my will.
Cherrystones for inner beauty and
Fertile currants to keep you.

Crushing.
Grinding.
Milling.
Pounding.

Round and round,
Until you love me.

Groovy
Michelle Hed

Groovy kind of love snuck up on me and
Really shook my soul and
Opened my eyes until
Only you would do for me and the
Vague recollection of what life use to be faded like a
Yawn in the morning breeze.

Road Trip

Patricia A. Hawkenson

We both heard it
hitting the windshield
with a tiny ping
not enough of a jolt
to take your eyes
off the road
or mine from the map.

By the time
we stopped for gas
and got back in the car
you noticed the light
from the growing crack.

S%*$!

Now were on a different road
watching that line
between us
growing deeper.

Seismic Shifts
RJ Clarken

A kiss:
that delicate
touch which signifies new
seismic shifts of deep emotion,
and heralds - something...but wait. Could it be
that love's tectonic plates move to
reveal an abyss? I
must rethink this:
No kiss.

Daisy I/II
Diana Terrill Clark (Domino)

Daisy I

She plucked the daisy
twirling it in her fingers
eyes half-glazed with love
wondering
did he love her too?

"He loves me
he loves me not..."
and so she plucked the
petals
one
by
one
until:

"He loves me!!"

In giddy glee she danced
across the field
into her home
where she dreamt
sweetly and
deeply
beneath
the night's stars.

Daisy II

The daisy waited,
breath bated,
wondering
would she notice him today?

And then—
Suddenly, he was away
from the earth
from his roots;
his stem apart
from all that had so contained him.
He hardly noticed the pain,
for
She had noticed him!

She loves me! the
daisy exulted!
Until
the Plucking began.

One
by
one
the petals
were painfully pulled,
discarded,
and each petal
hurt
more than the last
until
there were no petals
remaining.

Just the empty
drained stem.
Discarded
on the ground.

Speaking of Love
Laurie Kolp

A symphony shrills behind the storm doors,
Unlit bulbs emblazon winter's gray,
New life pops up in the barren fields;
Spring's resurrection loves this way.

Invitation to Love/Anti-Love
Barbara Ehrentreu

The invitation came
wrapped in the shape
of a young man
whose lips were my candy
and his body my playground
and I melted into him
for the rest of my life.

Anti-Love
Why do I need you?
You are a headache
shaped as a man.
I cannot be the person
you wish me to be
Yet you continue
to push me toward
an unwanted goal

You put your love away
in a suitcase
a long time ago
and threw away the key
Now all I see in your eyes
are indifference
and impatience.

Those hazel eyes I once spent hours
knitting a sweater for
in emerald green to match
the color your
eyes become when
you wear green
Those eyes that now
bore into me and hold
recriminations instead of love
Eyes that accuse me of faux crimes
made up by you.

I have grown tired of your cold face,
the frowns, the
loveless looks.
Your wrath
has eaten my love.
(2010 by Barbara Ehrentreu, Barbara's Meanderings)

The Admirer

Bruce Niedt

O Dawn, you are truly a goddess of morn,
I celebrate the very day you were born.
Your lips, full and luscious, the dew on a rose,
your eyes, clearest blue, your cute button nose,
your hair, long and golden, as smooth as spun silk,
your skin alabaster and purer than milk.
When you talk I hear music, when you walk I see dance –
Oh please, dearest Dawn, won't you give me a chance?

So you are the guy hanging out near my yard,
leaving notes in my mailbox, scrawled over a card?
I know that you've followed wherever I'm walking -
There's a name for that pal, and they call it stalking.
I'll never be yours, that you can assume,
even if you've built me a shrine in your room.
I'm sorry for you and your mental disorder,
but back off – I just got a restraining order.

City of Love
Jane Shlensky

Take a lovely old wooden bridge
worn smooth by centuries of lovers walking
hand in hand, besotted with one another,
their happiness reflected in the finger
of lake below them, echoes of lamplight
coloring golden the water
where swans glide, necks entwined.
Add rail planters glorious with
cascading flowers, like falling tributaries
filling the lake of love.
Put a full moon in the sky, tinting
the world a warm blue,
and then add you and me, my love,
perfect,
until you kiss me and whisper,
"I could go for a schnitzel and brewsky."
Then I know that love is forgiveness.

Love Shouldn't Hurt Like That

Shannon Bo Lockard

Weeping,
she replays the dreadful event
violence unchecked,
unleashed,
unasked for.
As she describes the way he struck her,
each blow more severe but felt less.
Glimpsing her child in the corner,
slight frame cowering
eyes wide and nose red from crying,
his spell is broken.
The memory of her scared, scarred child
etched into her heart,
her mind,
her soul.
She packs their bags to leave,
they depart hand in tiny hand.
She doesn't need that man!

Doesn't Look Like Love, but Is/Looks Like Love, But Isn't
Buddah Moskowitz

Doesn't Look like Love, But Is (Love Poem)

The place reeked of sweat
and insecurity,
there was a twisted honor
in this verbal mosh pit,
as insult upon insult
piled higher and cut deeper.

Nothing was sacred;
one's skin eruptions
the size of one's genitalia
the supposed sexual performance
of one's mother,

the more stinging,
the better.

Years in the future
the women in our lives
would never understand
this humor,
this camaraderie,
this test.

"It just sounds
so mean, so negative."

We tempered each other
in the nastiest, most vicious
remarks
because the last thing
we wanted was
to see your pal
completely devastated
the day his boss called him
a fuck up
or his girlfriend
tried to impugn his
manhood.

We were in training,
toughening each other up
for the struggle
that seemed as inevitable
as our fathers'
quiet exhaustion.

Looks Like Love, But Isn't (Anti-Love Poem)

Completely unbound
by desire and passion
they shamelessly explored,
unaware, unconcerned
with anything or anyone else.

The surgical perfection
in his oiled Olympian musculature
glistened,
and every inch of her skin
had been powdered,
waxed and painted
to superhuman effect.

His rigid, oversized and
camera-ready member
didn't fail owing to
off-camera doses
of Viagra and amphetamine,
and she accepted him
into every pulsating, waiting,
pre-lubricated orifice with breathless
adoration and acquiescence.

Over and over,
with random, alternating camera angles,
anything human sounding
was drowned out by music
designed to mirror the repetition
and the scene's presumed excitement.

The makers stopped trying for
the pretense of exposition
or dialogue – it just got
fast forwarded past anyways.

Having seen what felt like
hundreds of these loops,
in retrospect,
I resent how they
hijacked my sense of who I was
and what I wanted,

because while I still had my virginity,
I let them steal my holiness,
and I wish I could get it back.

Enough and Not Enough
Jane Penland Hoover

There was time enough
To take a walk
To sip a drink
Even to listen to you read
That story you are writing

There was time enough
To organize my poems
To ask Ms Florence for her help
Even to answer your question
About that unrecorded check

There was time enough
For three trips to eat
A visit to the mail room
Even to listen to the old man
Rant about his breathy pain

Still there were four tasks
Left undone to
Be folded into tomorrow
When there will again be

Time enough for what I love
And insufficient minutes for
Dusting, ironing, sweeping,
Or clearing over-stuffed drawers.

Love And Paper Clips
Linda Evans Hofke

Looking for love is like
searching for a paper clip in the
abyss of one's junk drawer,
weeding through the hodge podge
of the undesired, the unsuitables
pushed to one corner as you
examine the leftovers in the pile.
Just when your patience fails,
when you contemplate admitting defeat,
it appears out of nowhere,
the light from the window shining on
it, crystal clear, brilliant, and you
grab hold of it, knowing it is
the one thing that will
hold the pieces together,
perfectly.

Intertwined
Amy Barlow Liberatore

You recall that fall
the two of us, soul to soul
Wholly ourselves
if only for that moment

Now you're safe
in your comfort zone
She thinks she is the only one
And that you yourself hung the moon
While I hang around here awaiting what where how when,
pondering then

I whisper in your heart, stroking your memory
tenderly drawing you back to me
Our love happened
because nothing else could

Flesh upon flesh
the heart of the matter
smattering of promises we knew were loving lies

And now here's your life: organized, precise, clockwork
Mine the jumble of a funny, frantic existence
Yet there remains the magnetic, eclectic tug
pulling you back to me
across miles of untouchable roadblocks

Our lives forever tangled, intertwined
Even apart, forever you're mine

© 2010 Amy Barlow Liberatore

79

I Am Not In Love
Iain Douglas Kemp

I am not in love

I am not in love with you
For that would be reckless
I am not in love with you for that
Would be foolhardy

You are too rich in heart
And spirit, too beautiful
For one as small as I to ever contain
So I am not in love with you

I am not in love with you
Although I quiver at the sound of your voice
And I cannot be in love with you although the sight
Of you weakens my knees

The distance now between us proves
That I am not in love with you
For surely if I were, I could never
Survive without you

But yet I live. In a world of tears
And cold empty rooms
That are bereft of your sweet warmth
No, I am not in love with you

I am not in love with you
Counting the minutes 'til your return
Checking the phone repeatedly for signal
Waiting breathless, not in love

I am not in love with you
The way you lift my heart to soaring heights
With just a sigh and soft girl giggle
I am not in love with you

I am patient, waiting timelessly
For you to know that you're not in love with me
Either and then in such endless bliss
We can not be in love together

Prompt 6

TYPE OF PERSON

Almost Elegy For Dean Young Written On The Inside Of A Windbreaker.
mike Maher.

When I first heard Dean Young
was having heart issues
I assumed they meant one of his metaphorical ones,
the one perhaps a bit too obsessed with Daffy Duck
or the one which sometimes hides behind abstractness
or the one filled up to the brim with loneliness and monkeys and odes.

I never thought they meant the literal one,
the one in need of a transplant because of a degenerative heart
condition,
the one that now cannot not walk a single city block,
the one with congestive heart failure due to idiopathic hypotropic
cardiomyopathy,
the one now operating at 8% capacity.

Necessary it is to die if you are a living thing
but by no means is it necessary to do it so ironically.
Perhaps the first diamond-heart transplant.
The first heart that lives forever
and does not lie,
a rock inside a raindrop inside a wolf.

Some theories state that God
chose the initial configuration of the universe
for reasons we cannot hope to understand,
others that the whole history of science
has been the gradual realization that events
do not happen in an arbitrary manner
but instead reflect an underlying order.

I would gladly give Dean Young
one of my own hearts
if it would not ensure
the inability to enjoy the poetry I would be preserving.

There is an entire chapter
dedicated to why we can't remember the future,
why you can't go off in a rocket ship
and return back to Earth shortly before you leave,
wormholes and the curvature of the universe.
The average Earthworm has five hearts.

When something becomes ash,
there's nothing you can do to turn it back
but you can sprinkle it over the ocean.

Breadline reactionaries

Daniel Ari

In the soup line, people are mostly quiet.
Every once in a while, someone clicks their tongue or sighs.
You see, now and then, a glance at a wrist,
though a watch is almost never there.

Nearly every day someone bursts
about the billionaires and how the government
had better leave them the hell alone to keep
the country running. The loudest argument:

No taxes. It's the principle of the thing.
In the dining room, there's never a drop left over.
The only difference between people is how fast they eat.
Some gulp everything in a long draught and look around

for more. Others eat to the last moisture
by half teaspoons to trick the body into feeling full.
Nobody leaves anything over. Someone bursts:
There isn't enough salt and the potatoes are bruised.

The soup is too wet, and if the government can send
a man to the moon, the least they could do is learn to cook soup.
We migrate to the welfare office next where tired, angry workers
call us lazy, sometimes out loud, sometimes silently.

The Preacher
Michelle Hed

He has a direct line
to the ear of God.
His ears must burn
with shameful secrets of others;
His ears must weep
with the sorrow of others;
His ears must sing
with the joys of others;
His ears must tremble
with the fears of others;
And when the preacher
has fears, worries, sorrow and joys,
whose ears burn for him?
Yes, God of course.
But the preacher is only human -
and not immune to the same
emotions that rocks our lives.
Hoping, if not our ears
then our arms burn, ache,
tremble and shake with joy
when our preacher needs
to be lifted.

A Lover
Paula Wanken

beautiful sunrise ~
dependable, radiant
always there for him

an orbiting moon ~
his focus remains on her
as her night watchman

heavenly bodies
complementing each other ~
the other's lover

Hot Lunch Lady
Patricia A. Hawkenson

Hot Lunch Lady

At night
instead of saying your prayers
do you lie awake
reading letters from tattle-tale mothers
whose ungrateful daughters
smeared toothpaste on the sink
or left dirty dishes on the counter?

Do you have a secret checklist
of torturous foods
worthy of the crimes accused
like piles of mystery meat
when unmade beds
hide dirty socks or week-old pizza?

I have seen your mustache twitching
when it tries to hide
your horseradish grin
as you relish in my agony.

May God have mercy
on your husband's soul.

Blowtorch
Anders Bylund

Have you seen what I can do?
Have you felt my flames?
Have you melted through and through
Shouting out my name?

I'll melt you and burn you
Twist you and turn you
You're in agony, I'm the source
I'll broil you and eat you
Spoil you and cheat you
I'm a white-hot blowtorch

I'm your poison, dark and sweet
I'm your guilty bliss
I'm the sin you will repeat
Tethered to my kiss

I'll melt you and burn you
Twist you and turn you
You're in pain and I'm the source
I'll broil you and eat you
Spoil you and cheat you
I'm a white-hot blowtorch

College Student
Connie Peters

Finals have been getting to her,
Russian tea and M & M supply—about out,
her bed—not slept in, candy machine—empty,
so she and her friends climb fire towers at midnight,
sled ride down icy sidewalks on stolen food trays,
wear false noses and mustaches to the donut shop.
College—does it truly prepare you for the real world?

Tailgater
Barbara Ehrentreu

What possesses you to ride so close
to my car's back bumper
as if you were hoping
to jump and land
wheels first ahead of me?

Like a dog pushing its nose
into your lap to get food
or a pat on its head
you keep inching forward
though my speed increases
you keep upping your pace.

The right lane is clear
yet you want my space
I know if I move
you will surge ahead
for a few miles, but then
you will find another
moving slower than you and
play the same life threatening tag

I have seen your next victim
clearing the way
for your lethal game
You must be the king
of all you survey
mustn't you?

Tailgater you are a stain on the road
Though the sad truth is you don't know it.

The People of the Second Chances
De Jackson

We are the ones
who've messed up and stressed out
and held doubt in our mouths like
a lozenge, relishing its acrid memory.

We have saidseendone things
no one would believe
past lives laid behind us
like some twisted black magic carpet
that somehow still led us

                                    here.

We have been
found
and we abound with an inexpressible
joy that can only come from being
rescued
pursued
adored.

We are the ones
who know what it's like to be loved
anyway
regardless
still
in spite of
completely
without limits.

We know grace
is amazing
and forgiveness
is free
and none of it's easy
but it sure beats going back.

We know that the heart
is a fragile and resilient
vessel
and that the sun shines
best
through the cracks.

Day Dreamer
Hannah Gosselin

Freedom found in flight of falcon.
Mesmerized by sound of wind against wings.
Your voice resounds, bouncing from cliff to cave
as you swirl and swoop against cloudless, blue sky.
You perceive from a distance and see so clearly.
Clarity that only height will bring.

TOM'S BEACH, Scène Fourteen: A View Inside Out
Marilyn Braendeholm

Tom's mother knew the doctors wrong,
of this she had few doubts. Her
love for Tom was strong and sure.
He wasn't broken, as they said.
He wasn't fragile, as she feared.
He was her Tom, and every word
spoken she knew he heard.
Her Tom was a universe
on to himself.

He's awoken by clattering
again. They're spinning,
those two busy toys of his.

... And today is his birthday ...

He calls one of the toys mum,
it looks like the letter B
set firmly upon skinny sticks.
The other one's called Da, it's
much bigger, fussing and fretting,
and Tom's fixated, listening
to its deep screechy, thumpy sounds.

Noise noise, his head echoes
with mum and Da, and it
shakes him out of bed.

... Cake and ice cream for breakfast ...

Tom stands detached, observing
shimmering shadows along
the edge of his hand. He often
brings his mum and Da toys stride
up short. He sees what he wants
to see, not more. He's the spark
in his own universe. Tom is
that sparkling speck of dust

in the sunlight, and he dances
with moon beams on the wall
when the house is asleep.

... and lit birthday candles. He doesn't like those ...

Tom twirls through words that curl like
the waves in his hair. He closes
his eyes, mesmerised by sparkling
colours and numbers splashing like rain.
And he counts 1-2-3. Tom counts
colours. Number sums are for counters,
and he's not a counter. He's a boy,
and he spins like a planet

as his throat strums the sound
of his name: Tom-Tom-Tom
His name is the beat of a drum.

... He'd wished for a bucket of stones ...

And his lungs bellow out the sound
of a trombone, as he hums
a staccato happy birthday song.
Tom casts his glance at the toy
he calls mum, and then he dashes
off arms linked with bright humming
colours and small running numbers,
a periwinkle and a whelk,

all of them chasing after waves
that kiss and hug the edge
of his beach – It's Tom's Beach.

... Adorned with smiley face stickers ...

Night Clerk
Buddah Moskowitz

Dale always worked
the Wednesday night shift
at the Gold Star Motor Lodge
off the freeway
close to her house.

He was old enough
to comb his hair into
a perfect Brylcreem part,
and he wore
an anachronistic red bow tie.

He looked as kind as a pastor
and as conservative
as an accountant.

Every Wednesday at 6pm
I'd check in
and there was Dale,

"Good evening, Mr. Moskowitz.
You need a single?"

Smiling,
I'd nod, trying not to be embarrassed.

He'd run my credit card.
I'd pretend to check my phone,
and avoid eye contact
if there were
other waiting for their rooms.

Handing me the key
he'd direct me to my room,
even though it was
the same one
I rented every Wednesday.

At 9pm
when she had to go back to her family,
I'd walk her back to her car and then
swing by the office to turn in my key,
love-tipsy and swaggering.

Dale would look up from his
crossword puzzle, smiling
like this was the first time.

"Checking out, sir?"
Again, I nodded.

"Well, we hope you'll come back
and stay with us again."

Perfect.
Friendly, but not familiar.

He must've seen my kind
a hundred times a month,

but he had enough
discretion and honor
for the two of us,

which was perfect
seeing as I had none myself.

Dreamer
Iain Douglas Kemp

The mind wanders
and words spill from the finger tips
but no-one reads them
no- one cares

The mind wanders
and visions fill the soul
but hopes are left unfulfilled
hopes are left in clouds

The mind wanders
and struggles fill the heart
but marches are never started
marches are saved for moors

The mind wanders
and fears overwhelm the spirit
but demons are never faced
demons stay buried inside

The mind wanders
and words are conjured
but the mind strays
the mind is...

...dreaming.

Thoughtful Hillbillies

a.m.trumble

RICK:
Hey Dick?

DICK:
Yea, Rick?

RICK:
See that sky roll on by? (points)

DICK:
...Oh, my...

RICK:
Don't i-t'almost makes yer wanner... cry?

DICK:
(Sighs) Yea, er die...

RICK:
I mean, don't-it makes yer wanner ask... why?

DICK:
Don't think(thoughtful)- Nope. Can't say I'd-wanner even try...

(both take a deep breath in)
(RICK exhales but DICK starts hacking and coughing)
(RICK slaps him on the back)

RICK:
Dick! Wha-happened?! Yer almost choked, why?

DICK:
Oh, Rick (coughs)... I think I swallerd-a fly!

Poet
Nancy Posey

Wearing her flowing poet's clothes,
gauzy, ephemeral, in monochromatic beige,
she walks to the podium clutching
her books, post-it notes like feathers
marking the pages she will read
in that singsong voice she's perfected,
ending always on a downward note,
the way all her professors and mentors read.
Her glasses perch on the end of her nose,
necessary but as much a part of the charade
as apples and pencils stenciled on denim jumpers
of kindergarten teachers everywhere.
The poems she'll read are ones she always reads,
when she knows the audience is filled
not with critics or fans but with students
there under duress or promise of extra credit,
salvation from less than stellar essays
on Wordsworth, Frost, and Keats.
Statutory poetry, she's heard it called,
forcing it on them for their own good,
cloaked in allusions she once blushed
not to recognize herself.

Prompt 7

LOCATION

In Poplar Street
Jacqueline Hallenbeck

In Poplar Street, three houses in,
resides a poet with a thousand dreams.
To be discovered outweighs the lot
and in this town that time forgot,
with anticipation and joy, she beams.

You cannot miss her, it's a sure thing.
With no GPS, your chances are slim.
She'll wait patiently, in that same blind spot
in Poplar Street.

A lover of words, a poet redeemed,
her work pure laughter and awe it brings.
Although it might be a pretty long shot,
she keeps the FAITH and is hopeful, somewhat,
her wishful cup full to the brim
in Poplar Street.

(Previously published in The Hudson Independent)

Paris
Cara Holman

We bow our heads
at la Tombe du Soldat Inconnu,
collect postcards at le Louvre
and stroll along la Rive Gauche
in the footsteps of Hemingway.
April, I say, isn't the best time
to be in Paris,
as inconsistent skies
pelt rain on us one moment
and smile upon us
with all the good will
of a benevolent parent the next.
But Paris, he murmurs,
isn't the worst place
to be in April.

At the Fortune Teller's Tent
RJ Clarken

"Your story's told. The cards? They speak.
I hope my meaning's not oblique,"
the fortune-teller said to me,
"but life is such a potpourri."
I sighed, with just a bit of pique.

"You'll meet someone with strong mystique
who seems quite nice but very sleek.
Your openness will be the key.
Your story's told."

Prognostication? Not unique.
"You're much too vague," was my critique.
But she insisted, "I foresee
that this is what shall be. Shall be.
It doesn't matter what you seek.
Your story's told."

Sicilian Towns
Salvatore Buttaci

I love the sound of Sicilian towns
Like Naxos, Noto, and Canicattí.
To read on a map cities like that:
Enna, Raffadali, Mussomeli.

My heart leaps high when I hear the cry
Of Mistretta, Messina, and Trapani.
I can't explain the effect of these names
Like Ribera, Favara, Licata Friddi.

Each one is a song that moves me along:
Comiso, Catania, Castel Termini.
Each one a prize I give to my eyes:
Menfi, Bronte, San Cataldo.

Castles and vines; Oh, Sicily mine!
Marsala, Castel Buono, Castroreale.
A rich history: each one dear to me:
Taormina, Alcamo, and Corleone.
Beyond the boot we find our roots
In Mazzarino, Pachino, and Barcellona.
What could compare to the cool mountain air
Of Prizzi, Nicosia, and Caltagirone?

And where can the sea more bluer be
Than in Cefalù, Palermo, and Porto Empedocle?
But the village most dear is the one I most cheer:
The paese about which I admit I'm most crazy:
Acquaviva Platani from where my family came.
I love the sound of those Sicilian names!

A Forest Primeval
Claudette J. Young

She has arrived with her warm spritely manner
To this place among pine-covered granite walls.
Green light sprawls throughout the dark cedar forest,
Permeating all but the strongest bright whites
Of Oceanspray and Trapper's Tea or shrinking
Pink mountain heather that hugs the forest's floor.

Trunks sized for giant's toothpicks spear sky's raiment
With arms swaddled in fronds delicate as ferns.
Emerald moss portrays socks keeping roots warm
While mushrooms play among the resulting folds.
So it is that Spring calls on Glacier's Cedars,
Ever ready with blossom, leaf, sparkling stream.

On Hampstead Heath

Andrew Kreider

On Hampstead Heath, we watched the golden light
bewitch and then seduce the coming night.
A space like this no lover wants to leave,
when there is so much magic yet to weave,
and so we walked home slowly, holding tight

and laughing, as we tried to write
the story of our future, just to fight
for one last memory we could retrieve
on Hampstead Heath.

That was the place, in black and white,
we promised it would be all right
to let each other go, and grieve
while many miles apart - and yet believe
that we would one day reunite
on Hampstead Heath.

Long Island
Barbara Ehrentreu

The smell of wild roses growing along the shoreline
announced the start of summer
I tilled the soil each spring
for my garden where bright red cherry tomatoes
and plump round beefsteak ones grew.
Baby carrots fresh from the soil and nasturtiums flowering nearby.

The girls played on the bricks,
tightrope walking along the edges
Singing and dancing while performing their productions.
The hammock hung between the dogwood trees
where I lay facing the sky
canopied with the fragrant leaves.

Wild strawberries grew in the grass of my backyard and when
I mowed the smell of wild onions surrounded me as the tall
grass tickled my legs. Along the fence the roses bloomed in
paint box colors. White flowers painted with
red as if brushed by an invisible artist.
On the side of the house
peonies grew in pink profusion. I'd cut them and bring them
straight to the sink. Their blooms held ants between the
petals. I'd run the water hoping not to flatten their beauty.

In front were the azalea bushes, white and pink bouquets
and the impatiens planted along the edge
mixing with purple hyacinths. In spring
the tulips grew in ordered rows.
Later in the summer the gladiolas would
tower over all with their trumpet shaped blooms
so heavy they would lean over.

I went past the house since we left.
The new owners pulled up the garden.
Replaced it with ground cover.
It's as if my life were erased and all I have
are half remembered memories
when my world was car pools, raking, mowing,
and planting a garden.
When mother was my job and wife
sat on the back burner.

Long Island, Suffolk county, Rocky Point
you live as the impression on the sand
stays after the tide ebbs on your beaches
where once we walked,
our bare feet leaving no impression
on the shifting sand.

Lilac Rd

a.m.trumble

I
Where you sit.
a bit-
on a curve;
what you deserve-
You are the deserted;
the desert peaks.
Just a steel blue box made of
rotting wood that squeaks,
but held together with cement,
you are overlooking your empire that you lament-
the orange, lemon, and avocado trees,
strangled by a heap of pitiful pot seeds.
You are an emblem of warm cognition
that could exist in either summer,
or fall's ignition.
The colors are ever the same.
Except I noticed when the lilac came-

II
Where he sat
batting away a gnat
on a curve,
with such nerve-
such a creep-
Sucking liquid evils into the deep,
And burying them into his valley's center.
bemoaning all the money that he lent-her
what social strategies dissemble that trash pile?
his just cause-a bleeding sickness in his smile
I should have known retreat meant war
and screaming litter: "worthless", "whore"
Now he knows from experience even the sweetest liars,
can not extinguish those brush-fires,
even his large blue blanket won't kill-it-dead-
He will still see slight flickers of yellow, orange, and red.
Those colors were always the same.
except every spring when the lilac came.

III
Where I sit;
think for a bit;
solemn like a toad
outside the general store on Lilac Rd,
Such memories are proof
it's the one with the yellow roof.
what a moment of peace
release-
I won't die-here-end-up-dead
I'll just sit here and light up another red
I'll take a bite out of a greasy Al Capone.
And you know you're gonna hear him groan.
And now he
will forever be
that dizzy fellow
Lost in the slight flickers of orange and yellow
And now those colors will never again be the same
because I wasn't there when the lilac came.

Ode to Atlanta
Jane Penland Hoover

This city, it is mine,
has been as long as time.

I ride six lanes with verve,
round the juncture of the curve,

looking down the length of Peachtree Street
past the years and stories sweet.

This is my home alone,
these buildings rising ever higher, the drone

of cars and more -- masterful these people milling
through noisy parks, green walks, card swiping,

rushing ever in or out or back. Today
they still the busy ones, unlike me, here at play,

dreaming of my city life, my well-steered view,
clearing trouble, passing, pointing out the way --

this place, the whole of it, Atlanta and its dogwoods, clean-up
crews,
its stretch in all directions, bluesy darkened clubs, its church hard
pews,

sunsets showing off above, skyline shadows falling, drivers slowing
--
all mine as much as wrinkled skin, and my fingers typing.

This city, it is mine,
will be as long as time.

New Models
Kim King

At the entrance of the closed auto dealership,
a hand-painted sign taped over the Chrysler
emblem welcomes sinners and worshippers
to weekly revival meetings in the showroom.

Rows of folding chairs replace gleaming trucks
and minivans that faced expansive windows
to the busy street-- panes reflecting pain and joy,
sacrificing Wednesdays for miracles at 7:30 PM.

Balm, Where I Sleep
Khara House

Sneak a peek through cotton
chink of lemon light,
kiting, drift. These sheets sooth
my reeling dreams, peel me gently

through shifting
blush of dew. Shivers rippling
like swarm of honeybees,
olive stream roll over, roar

foam and steal my roaming.
Reveries smooth over this hue
cream milky tea.
I sink

in this snow,
this river of warmth,
stoked and stirred
within my own fires.

Writing Workshop
Nancy Posey

Close your eyes, she told us,
and visualize your childhood home.

Imagine yourself waking in your own bed,
snug blankets, warm and familiar.

Look around, remember the pictures
on your wall, the closet door you shut
before climbing into bed, a hedge
against monsters hiding there.

Listen for sounds, your mother busy
in the kitchen, your father
rustling the paper as he reads,
his coffee cooling on the breakfast table.

Peer through the window over the sink
and see the swing set, the sandbox,
the neighbor's clothes line.

As I drift along, lost inside her voice
as she directs us, I realize the place
I see materializes like the place
of dreams, one house I knew
set in some other yard, around
the corner, a different town.

Like the Samaritan at the well
who honestly answered
I have no husband, having five,
I must admit, I have no home,
but instead, a string of houses.

My childhood memories fit
into moving boxes, so much
lost along the way-all, that is,
but the memories, the sounds,
the tastes, the smells.

Prompt 8

WATER

Little Sounds Americana
mike Maher.

Shakespeare has me beat 154 to 0
and neither number is likely to change.
I've forgotten so much, even the parts I don't remember.
I know when the squirrel is dangling
from the bird feeder because the chain clinks,
when it leaves because of the thud it makes jumping down to the deck,
but who am I to decide the feeder is for birds only,
no squirrels allowed?
Some neighborhoods make you
put up Christmas decorations.
Singers are given some artistic freedom
when reciting the national anthem
but it better end the same way
and be less than two minutes flat,
otherwise you get the hose.
It all seems so distinctive when it's taken apart
the carbon footprints of city squirrels,
the 1,100 solar company employees laid off in one day,
the graffiti disguised as artwork on the steel indie film door
or is it art disguised as graffiti?
The forecast calls for rain
but rain doesn't answer,
doesn't even get out of bed that morning,
not wanting to be called or told what to do and when to do it.
It's about time we started inventing new shapes,
almost isosceles trapezoid-rhombusgrams,
the mike Maher.-agon which has no ends
and is always on fire,
nothing equilateral.

A Glass Of Poetry

Jay Sizemore

If this poem were water
you could drink my words
and feel them blossom
in your stomach
like a warm shot of whiskey,
and your cheeks would flush
with color splotches
reminiscent of pink clouds
after a thunderstorm,
your body getting drunk
on emotions derived
from the power of
written language.

You could feel my thoughts
course through your veins
like some rough drug,
a rhinoceros crossed with
an elephant,
dragging its tusks
along the walls.

You could take my poem
and soak it in a rag
to gently wet the lips
of a man found in the desert
who looks just like me,
only he's not
and never will be
because the sun ate his skin
and bleached the personality
right out of his brain.

You could drown yourself
in a thimble full
of my love.

You could mix my love with sugar,
valium, chloral hydrate, phenergan,
and cyanide,
cherry flavored poetry
for the nine hundred
and nine people
willing to kill their children
and themselves
for revolutionary suicide,
martyrs
for communism
in the year I was born,
while you call the president
a fascist
for passing a bill
on health care reform.

You could pour my poem
into the powdered soil
of the potted flowers
your mother bought you
for Easter, orange daisies
jumping with vibrance
right out of the fabric
of ordinary life
like phosphorous flames,
then watch with growing disdain,
as they wither away to nothing,
or undergo a hideous
metamorphosis
into fetal pigs dangling
from the bright green stems,
wondering if their eyes will open
and ask you for milk.

I should have warned you,
my words are poison,
but it's too late,
you read them,
and you are seventy
percent water already,
and now there's an ocean
building inside you
that means to drown
the entire fucking world.

Partly Cloudy, Looks Like Rain
Cara Holman

The weatherman says
we can expect rain.
The weatherman says
that a cold and vigorous
storm system is forming
in the Pacific and
will move inland
causing precipitation
and unseasonably low
snow levels.
There's even a chance
of thunderstorms.

I sip my tea
and watch the sky change
as these Pacific-induced,
rain-laden clouds
move towards their destiny.

Roar

Anders Bylund

From where I stand I can smell the ocean, or rather,
I can smell decaying seaweed on the red tide washing over desert-
white sands.
Everywhere around me, people shuffle their feet and scrape along,
making do with whatever they can grab and whoever they can get,
drummers in the summer toning down to pitter-patter of pithy little
ticks to make it to the next milepost on the road of survival,
who kill for a nickel to blow on cocaine and strippers in Vegas or
Caracas or the carnival in Rio,
who run from the ghosts up close and far anon, morose on a double
dose of magic powder on toast,
who sprawl like Southern kudzu over villages and cities with a
firehose of   bulldozers, and the composer is a poser getting closer
to pure nothing,
who cry over lost souls of teachers and tadpoles, from the equator
to the North Pole where the trolls all dig for coal,
with nothing left to lose but the mud caked on their shoes and
she'll refuse to be your muse until you give her some excuse,
and nothing more to say if you portray him in a way reeking of hair
spray and dismay, beaten down by a bouquet of steel magnolias,
who put their ideals on the market with a spark of dark, Utopian
dreams to tease forgiveness from an indifferent universe,
who yank and tear at the edges of a wayward poem, uncredited,
unknown, pouring blood off the sides and sweat too, crazy blend of
higher diction and lower voices and
nothing is sacred but sacrosanctity itself -- nor even that,
who create a tiny spot for themselves in the miasma of unforgiving
chaos.

And from where I stand, the water looks warm.

123

Water Acrostic
Laurie Kolp

Waves breathing in and out
An occasional water spout
Taste of salt in the air
Eyes strained from the glare
Refreshing water everywhere

God's Spectrum
S.E.Ingraham

watering the winter
scorched lawn
she is careful
to shoot the road grit
back out to the curb
and scoop the dog cigars
into a bucket
when she is suddenly
blinded by a rainbow
in the spray

transfixed, she can't
seem to move
just stares
at the perfect miniature
mere inches beyond
the hose nozzle

she feels inexplicably
reverent as if she
should kneel down,
offer thanks
when it hits her;

it's Good Friday
that holiest of days
and she all at once
feels like praying

The Swimmer

a.m.trumble

Once her legs had grown long enough
and strong enough, she earned that first moment of exultant
bliss-

With toes at the edge, cleaving the concrete, she relinquished to an
unknown world. Not just a slight quiver, but a tyranny-eluding full
body tremor in which her air was transfixed with nothingness-

And for an age, it seemed, she had been flanked by the smooth,
cool waters.
Enveloped by it's other-worldly and molecular sovereignty. Her
lungs full, and still filling, she is no longer,
amiss.

(The champion swimmer has drowned.
She is stuck down somewhere in the drain.
She collects silently amongst the foul
"Chlorophyllic"-idyllic, green-blue algae blossoms. But she, ever so
stick-like and frail, has been washed out before the red had left the
bloom.)

What If The Bathtub Floods The World & Drags Humanity Down The Drain
Nikki Markle

Water
Trickling from the
Tap,
Not too hot and
Not too
Cold,

Rising up the
Porcelain wall,
Streaming over to
Rush down the other
Side.
Slithering

Across the
Tile,
Filling the
Floor like a
Pool at high
Tide.

On and
On,

Attracting droplets,
Expanding,
Extending.

People
Perching on
Rooftops or

Clinging to
Ornately carved
Headboards,

Legs
Churning the lukewarm
Liquid
Fusing together,

Lungs sucking in
Moisture,
Gills forming along
Ribcages,

Until

Someone
Swims down to
Pull the small rubber
Plug.

With The Flow
Janet Rice Carnahan

Water as life's teacher,
Flows freely along,
Carrying life with it,
With speeds reflecting our heart!

Rushing forward in leaps and bounds,
Cascading towards resistant boulders,
Going any way it pleases,
Water as life's teacher!

Stagnant ponds wait,
Algae and slime collect.
Until clear and clean motion,
Flows freely along,

Barely a dribble visible,
Slowed to a trickle of sound,
Drop by drop, hardly a pulse,
Carrying life with it!

Frozen still in place,
Ice and snow can melt,
Moving into springs we hold dear,
With speeds reflecting our heart!

Antediluvian

De Jackson

long before the
tears
fears
promises
lies,
way before the
world cracked open
she
doodled in the margins
watched her p's & q's
turned face to the sun
loved
laughed
lived
and kept at least one foot
on dry land at all times.

now
breath held
lungs bursting
current strong
she sinks
until she can no longer see
the blurred edge
where she ends
and ocean begins.

Water Of Life
Iain Douglas Kemp

(i)   Birth to Youth

Bursting, bubbling on to the scene,
struggling through the rocks and shocks
of infancy, rushing fast as the wind
into the helter-skelter madcap adventure
of adolescence

(ii)   The Middle Course

Calmer now, the hard fight is won,
sights set on far distance, the long haul:
steady as she goes, winding on, running smooth,
the pace is even, the course is plain,
twists and turns passed with the ease
of maturity

(iii)   The Sedimentary Passage

The end in sight, all haste is lost,
left behind are the deposits of wisdom
and experience, memories now:
the final course is smooth,
time, ever the enemy slows the pace,
the run to the sea that is not death but a new life
of eternity

Waterbird
Khara House

Water, rippling, dancing on its own back,
rolling and licking and hemming the earth in.
Anticipating the teal, the ibis, the gull—
skimming, swiftly, standing still.

The water is more of me than I am of teal.
Lets me in, and is in me. Flecks across my face—
water is the most tender lover. Drowning
is becoming more of myself than my body can handle.
Water never forgets I am here. Never forgets
my face. Never leaves me.

Suspense
Sara Vinas

A simple splash
Becomes
Freeform art
Airborne
Hydrogen and
Oxygen bonds
Hold fast
For just a moment
Then
Break
Into thousands of
Sunlit sparkles
Before they
Dip and dive
Leaving only
Concentric memories

Prompt 9

ALL I WANT

All I Want Is My Hair To Grow Back

Salvatore Buttaci

You think me shallow because in a world
of things I should want I point to my head
and say I want my hair to grow back
You would expect me to say millions
of dollars or youth or Clark-Gable looks
or Methuselah's secret to very long life,
But I want the hair on my head to grow back.
It's a simple request: to restart those follicles
that for years remain dormant or dead
beneath the surface of a pink skull
stubbled with fine white hairs you could count,
a white billiard ball smooth as a baby's behind,
a head bald as a baseball concealed under a baseball cap.
All I want is my hair to grow back,
to wake up and see reflected in the bathroom mirror
a new man with a shock of thick hair--
the color doesn't matter!--a new man with hair shoots,
like stalks of wheat come harvest time in Kansas,
a new man who can throw his hat away,
feel young again, live forever in the hairy moment,
feel richer than a king, stronger than Sampson
before Delilah snipped his--all I want is my hair
my hair my hair my hair my hair to miraculously
GROW BACK!

All I Want Is Pancakes For Breakfast
Diana Terrill Clark (Domino)

All I want is pancakes for breakfast
And sausage with a bit of the syrup
accidentally
on it.

All I want is pancakes for breakfast
And blueberries in them
bleeding purple
juice.

All I want is pancakes for breakfast
and a rose on the table
and that warm flower
scent.

All I want is pancakes for breakfast
and you sitting there
eating them
with me.

All I Want Is To Be Left Alone
Bruce Niedt

All I want is to be left alone –
Don't call me from my evening meal.
Keep all the beggars off my phone;
all I want is to be left alone.
I hardly ever leave my home,
so spare me the shady timeshare spiel.
All I want is to be left alone –
Don't call me from my evening meal.

(Previously published in Tilt-a-Whirl as "All I Want")

All I Want Is One More Morning

Jane Penland Hoover

I awake as light spills in
hear water splash the basin
and imagine your attention
to your face, lathering to shave

I curl around my pillows
draw yours closer, listen
as your wing-tip shoes brush
the plush beige rug

Morning sleepy head, you say
and bend to give a kiss
as I rush a smile into your wide embrace
press my palm into your
yellow tie, downy touch.

Ready for your morning meeting
yet
you're not moving toward the door...

Later
after you are gone
I know that should I have a million days
ten million nights, I will forever
know the touch of yellow silk

All I Want (A Rondeau)
Linda Evans Hofke

All I want is to turn back time.
Is that wish really such a crime--
to want to feel your touch once more
the way it used to be before
back when we were still in our prime?

Those yesteryears, they were sublime,
with endless passion all the time,
promises of forevermore.
All I want is to turn back time

to when love blossomed like Springtime,
fireworks burst and bells would chime.
I was the one you did adore
before you shut and locked the door.
When did your love turn on a dime?
All I want is to turn back time

All I Want Is A Dream And A Cape

Khara House

and a boat. To sail away in. Or
reach the stars like yesterday's passing.
And a cup of red tea, and threads of saffron
and rusted love poured over me

like honey. And a piece of the moon,
and a star to watch over it. Or a carnival
balloon, to sail away in.

Or a cake baked in cream soaked
cardamom. A portion for the world
and a slice for me. To sail away in. And a day,
and a dollar not to spend. A walking

refrain, and a map of Spain. And the river
Jordan. And a mask to hide away in,
and a piece of you, to steal away.

I REALLY, REALLY want.
(ZZZZ AH!)
Michele Brenton

I don't want riches,
diamonds you can keep.
You can stuff
your chocolates.
Please just let me sleep.

I don't want gifts of roses
even if they're red,
stick 'em where
the sun don't shine,
I just want my bed.

I'm telling you plainly
what I'd love you for best;
let me sleep,
just let me sleep
and to hang with the rest.

Prompt 10

AFTER LEAVING HERE

After Hearing The News
Jay Sizemore

he will wipe his tears away,
he will walk out of this office,
out of this hall, out of this building,
climb into the oven-baked warmth
of his vehicle and roll the windows down,
turn the rock n roll up so the bass drum
rattles the loose CD's stashed in the door,
while driving fast enough that the wind
ripping though his hair brings back memories
of summer days in cars without air conditioning.
He will not cry again, will not tell a soul
what the man in the white lab coat read
from the sheet of paper in the plastic clip board,
but will go home and hug his wife,
will let his cat curl into his lap and purr
while the television blares out background noise
for serenity. He'll make plans to visit family,
to visit friends, some near, some forgotten,
to see concerts of bands he has always wanted to see,
but never had the time. He'll marvel
at just how healthy he feels. He'll lie down to sleep,
in sheets crowded with scents of nights
before this one, each one seeming new,
and he will wait for his eyes
to adjust to the darkness.

Gone
Michelle Hed

After I am gone,
my body burned to ash -
Will I cross through
your pearly gates
and be infused with the wisdom
of the ages, past and present?
Existing on another plane,
seeing old friends,
ancestors,
companions –
Will I have something to do?
A worthwhile pursuit?
Will feelings of hate,
fear and anger leave me?
Will I be the embodiment
of all my best qualities?
After I am gone...

Lost and Found
Jane Shlensky

"Found dead" the Key West police report said,
a phrase that sits in my head,
spinning details and questions.
Who found you? Why and when?
Foe or friend? Natural or lost causes?
Were you in love with cocaine again
or just alone and stricken,
your poor tired heart done
with earthly confusion?
Were you working again,
making beautiful pictures
of sunsets and birds in flight,
beach pools and thundering waves,
blues of horizons meeting seas?
Did you see the people
who love you despite everything,
their faces rising like fog in the swamps
calling to you, holding you, laughing with you,
needing your chortle and crow?
I think of a costume party when
I was Muffet and you were a shark
I mistook for a sperm, having missed
your sagging dorsal fin, and
how you mauled me
and laughed that singular laugh.
I try without success to recall
our last words to one another,
but I know they were
see you later, hang in there,
remember who you are words
that bear frequent repeating.
I would have said I love you
and you would have said, me too,
for that was our ritual,
but would you have known
that I meant it, that I always
found such good in you?
I know you sought meaning
and purpose in life, to somehow
reclaim your children's esteem
and the joy of your youth.
Did you find peace
before you were found
dead?

For The Love Of Writing
Claudette J. Young

Roads' stripes entice us onward,
Always toward adventure ahead.
Will Wanderlust release our hearts
For rest and surcease from homeless
Days and nights under leaden skies?
Maps tell little of travel's truth,
None of weather's precociousness.
Where will this perverse imp of Muse
Lead us when all is spent, gone?

I'm Not Going Anywhere.
Michele Brenton

I'm not
leaving here
so there's no reason to write
and say goodbye.
So I won't.
I've put my words
on the page
of your site
and I've left myself
in them all
and you might
think there is an after
but there isn't
there is only now
and here I am
and here I'll stay
you can't get rid of me
that easily!

After Leaving Here - I Will Be There

Pearl Ketover Prilik

After

wrapped moon-silvered and glimmering
listen and hear the collective chorus sing in
gathered crescendoed filaments from a street still simmering
with the heat of past passion drifting in the soft night breeze
the music of Muse call ripples down the dusky avenue each to
another
on that wet cobblestoned street, emptied and departed, washed in
living
lyrics - sweet, painful, searing, soul seizing
wispy, wafting, fragments lift shimmering with soft light
as the last poet walks with slow steps alone into the darkening
night

Leaving

sole foot-falls indelibly rising from glistening ground
to meet with the others, for truly leaving this place, though
challenges concluded
shall never be, once Muses have met, dance and dipped, each slips
into the archival ever of the glowing after leaving ever-present
glimpsed in the rustle of leaves on a soaring oak
in the tumultuous shower of white chestnut blossoms
on the glistening of that forever wetted cobblestoned street

Here

as the wind sings of all that was, and remains, in the breath of
poets past, present and those that will come to walk for a while and
leave
footfalls in the mist, whispers riding the wind

After leaving ..

THE POETIC ANTHOLOGISTS

Daniel Ari
Michele Brenton
Salvatore Buttaci
Anders Bylund
Janet Rice Carnahan
Diana Terrill Clark (Domino)
RJ Clarken
Barbara Ehrentreu
Hannah Gosselin
Michael Grove
Jacqueline Hallenbeck
Patricia A. Hawkenson
Michelle Hed
Linda Hofke
Cara Holman
Jane Penland Hoover
Khara House
S.E. Ingraham
De Jackson
Elizabeth Johnson
Iain Douglas Kemp
Kim King
Laurie Kolp
Andrew Kreider
Catherine Lee
Amy Barlow Liberatore
Shannon Bo Lockard
mike Maher.
Nikki Markle
Buddah Moskowitz
Bruce Niedt
Connie L. Peters
Nancy Posey
Pearl Ketover Prilik
Jane Shlensky
Jay Sizemore
a.m.trumble
Sara Vinas
Paula Wanken
Claudette J. Young

The Poets Speak
Bios and Acknowledgments

Daniel Ari

Daniel Ari is a poet, writer, performer, musician, writing teacher and copywriter in California's Bay Area. He has recently published work in Conscious Dancer, Writer's Digest, McSweeney's and Ceramic Arts & Perception as well as on the blog he shares with Marna Cosmos, IMUNURI.blogspot.com.

Daniel Ari's Strand:
and the tongue is a mighty and delicate muscle when it moves the pen or takes the wheel

Michele Brenton

Born in Swansea, South Wales, Michele Brenton shares her birthday and birthplace with another Swansea poet, Dylan Thomas. She spent some time living on the Greek island of Kefalonia as did another poet, Lord Byron. She has lived longer than they managed and been happily married for twenty-one years during which time she (with some help from her long-suffering husband) produced a remarkably talented son who will far outstrip her creatively. She writes poetry and is delighted, surprised and honored each time her work is included in a publication. It happened first in 2001 when her poem Enemies got into the When the Teacher Isn't Looking anthology published by Pan Macmillan and most recently in 2011 with the inclusion of her poem The House in The Spirit of Poe anthology published by the Landmark Literary Press.

Three books of her seven book series the Alternative Poetry Books (the Yellow edition, Pink edition and Blue edition) have been published by Endaxi Press so far and can be found fleetingly from time to time in the Amazon poetry bestsellers lists. As banana_the_poet she was voted the most popular human poet by the Twitter community in the Shorty Awards 2011.

She can be found on Twitter as @banana_the_poet and on Facebook as MichelePoet

Michele Brenton's Strand:
A persistent itch at the back of my brain.

Salvatore Buttaci

Salvatore Buttaci is an obsessive-compulsive writer who lives in West Virginia with his wife Sharon. He was the 2007 recipient of the $500 Cyber-wit Poetry Award. His poems, stories, articles, and letters have appeared widely in publications that include New York Times, U. S. A. Today, The Writer, Writer's Digest, Cats Magazine, The National Enquirer, Christian Science Monitor, Thinking Ten, Pen 10, and Six Sentences. His latest collection of short-short fiction, 200 Shorts, is available in book and Kindle editions at Amazon.com. You can read more of Salvatore's Buttaci's work at: http://salvatorebuttaci.wordpress.com and http://salbuttaci.spruz.com
Salvatore Buttaci's Strand:
I write to hush the longings in my soul

Anders Bylund

Anders Bylund is a freelancer in financial journalism, technology, music, and poetry. His day job at The Motley Fool lets him sprinkle his stories with poetry every April. You've never lived until you enjoyed a Villanelle about the stock market.
Anders Bylund's Strand:
The loves of my life -- all the laughter and cries

Janet Rice Carnahan

An amusing and rich collection of experience influenced Janet's love of poetry. Most certainly, it included listening to an Irish grandmother tell her rapid fire limericks, a humorous father who loved the written and spoken word, a mother who wrote playful poetry for friends, a neighbor who generated endless puns and her own enjoyment reading children's books to her children, Courtney and Scott. After a career as an early childhood educator and owning a preschool for years, Janet started writing poetry after being further inspired by the likes of Dr. Seuss, Ogden Nash, Shel Silverstein and Robert Louis Stevenson. Loving the rhythm and rhyme, Janet felt poetry best summed up life in sweet sound bytes that invite in and frame captured moments of life's perfection. Poems speak their own language, tell their own tales and offer snapshots of life from each uniquely crafted perspective; an endless beauty in motion. Currently, she is developing and co-editing a web site with her husband, Bruce, which will include poetry and photography. She was encouraged to write by family and friends, namely a father at her preschool, Skip Hansen, who left amusing poems on her desk, awaiting a humorous reply. Most recently, her inspiration has come from the talented poets on the Poetic Asides blog by the senior editor for Writer's Digest, Robert Lee Brewer. She is grateful for the opportunity to be part of the beautiful growing community found on his blog. For example, Robert presented a variety of poetic forms allowing the poets to explore different styles. This served to expand Janet's perspective on the written art, further enhancing her ongoing delight in poetry!
Janet Rice Carnahan's Strand :
It begins as a whispered vision until it glistens in the sun of reality.

Diana Terrill Clark

Diana is a legal secretary with more hobbies than she knows how to handle. She loves her job, yet there are so many other things vying for attention: She writes and has completed her first novel about a psychic detective whose encounters with bad guys of all description include a few with supernatural powers. She writes poetry, sews historical costumes, bakes, knits, crochets and embroiders, and has raised three boys to be lively upstanding men who visit as often as they can. She lives with her husband and cats in Scottsdale, Arizona, and hopes to retire to a greener pasture someday; as long as no hobby is left behind, she'll be good. You can find some of her work at her blog, "Drift of Bubbles" at dianaterrill.wordpress.com.

Diana Terrill Clark 's Strand:
A skein, a web, a snarl of words gently untwists and becomes something beautiful

RJ Clarken

RJ Clarken is a writer, poet, photographer and graphic artist with an offbeat sense of humor. Her work has been published in Writer's Digest, Möbius, Asinine Poetry, USA Today Online, Sol Magazine, Vermeer, Postcard Shorts and Trellis Magazine, among others. She is the Editor of Goldfinch, the literary journal of Women Who Write, a NJ not-for-profit women's writing collective. She is also the author of Mugging for the Camera, a quirky, oddball, humorous book of poetry and Penny Wishes, a young adult novel. Some of RJ's "stuff" can be found at http://1ightverse.blogspot.com

RJ Clarken's Strand:
If you can say everything you need to say in just 17 syllables - and make people laugh in the process - you are a true success.

Barbara Ehrentreu

Barbara, a retired teacher with a Masters degree in Reading and Writing K-12 and seventeen years of teaching experience, lives with her family in Stamford, Connecticut. Besides writing she enjoys cooking and baking and walks along the shore where she can observe egrets and swans. She has been writing poetry since third grade. When she received her Masters degree she began writing seriously. If I Could Be Like Jennifer Taylor, Barbara's first published YA novel, just published September, 2011 by MuseItUp Publishing, was inspired by Paula Danziger. Barbara is a NY Literature Examiner for Examiner.com with several articles for them. Her blog, Barbara's Meanderings: http://barbaraehrentreu.blogspot.com is networked on both Facebook and Blog Catalog. She hosts Red River Writers Live Tales from the Pages every 4th Thursday. In addition, her children's story, "The Trouble with Follow the Leader" and an adult story, "Out on a Ledge" are published online. She writes book reviews for Authorlink.com, and several of her reviews have been on Acewriters and Celebrity Cafe. She is a member of SCBWI. Writing is her life!

Barbara Ehrentreu's Strand:
Words rush from my fingers when the spark of my muse is ignited.

Hannah Gosselin

Hannah Gosselin is perpetually inspired by the love shared with her husband and their two young sons and is awestruck by the beauty in nature. She enjoys indulging in the heart-work of writing, dance and the visual arts. Hannah was awarded a diploma by the Institute of Children's Literature located in West Redding, Connecticut, for the successful completion of the course: "Writing for Children and Teenagers," on April, 19th, 2010. One may contact her on Facebook, if they so please.

Hannah Gosselin's Strand:
A creative welling up occurs within my being brought on by a scrim of flowing silk, bit of red ribbon, speckled stone, cobalt colored marble, fragment of pale aqua sea glass, bounce of wind in the end of a pine bough, joy sparkling in one's eye; language of love, surging in my blood, settling in my bones; overflowing in my spirit and causing a hunger, a need to respond.

Michael Grove

Michael Grove is a lifelong resident of Mid-Michigan. He is a writer and lyrical poet with a pure and simple style that comes from his heart and touches the soul. He has been writing hopeful and spiritually uplifting verse since he was 10 years old and dabbles at putting some of his poetry to music. He has published the first book of a three-book series, "Observations: The 1st Four Dozen" and has completed "Observations: The 2nd Wave". Current projects include a faith-based poetry collection as well as a novel. His work experience includes college instructor, homebuilder, real estate broker and operations manager of a mortgage company. Mike appreciates spending quality time with his two children as well as his dog, Jake.

Michael Grove's Strand:
With pen in hand I'll take a stand and sing of love from up above.

Jacqueline Hallenbeck

Jacqueline Hallenbeck is a Poet-in-Transit. Author of "Poem-atic", a book of 109 very short, very entertaining poems, and five chapbooks: "Poetry is... ", "Poesía es...", "Faith in the City", "Tine after Tine", and "Random Poetry (these bullets don't hurt)". Her work has appeared in Current/The Hudson Reporter, Margen Cero, Ecuatoriano and The Hudson Independent, among others. She is the US distributor of a magazine out of UK called Turbulence. She reads her pieces at open mics whenever opportunity arises. For more on her work, visit her website:
 http://www.angelfire.com/sd2/sadsam/index.html.

Jacqueline Hallenbeck 's Strand:
Emptying out my brain's contents, one poem at a time.

Patricia A. Hawkenson

Patricia A. Hawkenson is the author of 'Magnetic Repulsion, 100 Poems from Desire to Disgust.' It is available at: http://outskirtspress.com/webpage.php?ISBN=9781432748548.

She is a National Board Certified Language Arts instructor in Eau Claire, WI and has won various awards for innovation and use of technology in education. Patricia enjoys many artistic expressions such as: stained glass, sewing tapestry handbags, and illustrating with watercolor pencils. Her poetry blog, Expressive Domain, contains hundreds of her poems. Enjoy them here:
www.phawkenson.edublogs.org.

Patricia A. Hawkenson's Strand:
Gossamer strands of understanding stick until I weave them into what they were meant to feel.

Michelle Hed

Michelle Hed is a photographer, poet and artist living in Minnesota. Michelle finds her art with every glance out her window and every step out her door. She is happiest when she is outside with a camera in her hand. Her poems have appeared in the following books and online journals *A Handful of Stones, Pay Attention: A River of Stones, Haiga Online,* and was a finalist in the *Poetic Asides Poem a Day Challenge 2009.* Her photography has been awarded in local contests and has been published in *Minnesota Birding* and the newly released *Holiday Word Gifts.* She also has a book, *Natural Musings,* which contains both her photography and poetry. She maintains a blog, www.thepenlensandbrush.blogspot.com for all her artistic endeavors. She is married to her best friend, has two beautiful daughters and two mischievous hounds.

Michelle Hed's Strand:
Nature captured by my eye, makes my pen move.

Linda Hofke

Linda Hofke holds a B.S. in Elementary Education from Kutztown University. Though a Pennsylvania native, Linda has lived in Germany for over a decade. She teaches English as a Foreign Language and maintains two blogs: http://lindas-life-otos.blogspot.com and http://lind-guistics.blogspot.com. She is currently working on two book projects.

Linda Hofke 's Strand:
A sight or sound, taste or smell, feeling or thought; in everything and anything, my muse can be found.

Cara Holman

Cara Holman lives with her family in the Pacific Northwest, where she finds abundant inspiration for her poetry in the natural surrounding. These days, she focuses mostly on haiku and other related forms. Her haiku and haibun have been featured in Four and Twenty, Frogpond, The Heron's Nest, Notes From the Gean, Sketchbook, Riverwind 30, the World Haiku Review, and VoiceCatcher 6. She recently received the First Prize 2011 Porad Award, a Sakura Award in the Vancouver Cherry Blossom Festival Haiku Invitational 2011, and Third Prize in the 2011 International "Kusamakura" Haiku Competition. She blogs at Prose Posies: http://caraholman.wordpress.com

Cara Holman 's Strand:
From prompt to pen to page, an unbroken path of poetry or prose--it's all good!

Jane Penland Hoover
Jane Penland Hoover grew up in Decatur, GA, and graduated from Emory University with BBA. After her husband suffered a stroke in 1973, Jane began a 25 year career with Clairmont Oaks, Inc., operating and constructing senior housing communities. In 1992, after her daughters graduated and married, Jane founded memoir writing groups in Athens and Greensboro, GA, before moving to NC in 2011. Today she leads writing workshops, writes poetry, publishing in several anthologies, and delights in her daily photography. http://jpenstroke.wordpress.com/
Jane Penland Hoover's Strand:
morning walk beneath blue sky, whirr of dragonfly, scent beyond my eye

Khara House
A Pennsylvania-native living in Arizona, Khara Elizabeth House received her Bachelor's Degree in English from Messiah College. After a deliciously dull and unintended year off from academic pursuits, she earned her Master's Degree in Creative Writing from Northern Arizona University, where she now teaches in the English Composition program. To learn more about her, including her frequent voyages into the Nation of Procrasti, visit her blog at http://ourlostjungle.blogspot.com
Khara House 's Strand:
This world is a lost jungle, just longing for us to paint its walls with carefully inked leaves.

S.E.Ingraham
S.E.Ingraham has written poetry for most of her life and is happiest when her work reflects some of the other passions in her life: sanity, social justice, and family. Some recent successes include being selected to attend the Colrain Manuscript Publishing Conference, plus publication in Pay Attention: A River of Small Stones and on-line in A Handful of Stones. Ingraham continues to work assembling a web-page http://www.baring-witness.com/ and some of her poetry can be found on the blog http://thepoet-tree-house.blogspot.com/
S.E. Ingraham 's Strand:
Sometimes out of the darkness of the soul; sometimes, skimmed from the lightest part of everything - words to hammer and twist and weave until they make sense or don't - poetry saves me, is the best and the worst of me.

De Jackson

De Jackson is a parent, a poet and a Pro Crastinator of the highest order. Her muse is a mermaid, migrating between Lake Tahoe and the ocean. She's a terrible housekeeper, mean Scrabble player, and hopes someday to live up to this lofty job description: I'll be the poet who sings your glory, and live what I sing every day. – Psalm 61:8. You can read more of her at whimsygizmo.wordpress.com.

De Jackson 's Strand:
She is prompted by the promise of phrases flung into the wind and the prospect of watching them fly.

Elizabeth Johnson

Elizabeth Johnson is a full-time homemaker, part-time coffee drinker, and occasional wordsmith. She is in love with her Savior and her husband, and spends her free time composing poetry and devotionals, creating greeting cards, and concocting recipes from scratch. Her poetry has appeared in Writer's Digest and other nonprofit publications, and can also be found at http://dandeliondigest.blogspot.com.

Elizabeth Johnson 's Strand:
Sculpting beauty with words, as the world was beautifully formed by the great Creator's words.

Iain Douglas Kemp

Iain Douglas Kemp lives and works in Southern Spain. He has been writing for over 30 years. He considers himself a poet first and a teacher second. He is also a singer/songwriter and plays drums and harmonica. Publishing credits include the poem "Peregrine" being recorded for podcast on the 'Born Free Foundation' web site by actor and animal welfare activist Virginia McKenna. His website www.iainkemppoetry.com showcases over 100 of his poems and publishes a new podcast poem every Friday. He also gives regular readings in his home town in Spain. He is a member of the on-line poetry group "The Baker's Dozen" with whom he writes regularly in between his busy schedule as a teacher of English as a foreign language.

Iain Douglas Kemp 's Strand:
The sands of time are just made of sand but the water of life touches every soul

Kim King

Born in Lockport, New York, Kim King graduated from the University of Buffalo with a BA and MEd. in French. She studied for a year in Grenoble, France, and teaches French at Cedar Cliff High School in Central Pennsylvania. Her love affair with poetry began as a child when she started writing in elementary school, but she began writing seriously after the death of her beloved father, Kurt, in 2002. Kim "met" many of the anthologists in April 2009 when she entered Robert Brewer's Poetic Asides PAD challenge. In both 2009 and 2010 challenges, one of Kim's poems was selected as one of the top 50. She has won several poetry contests and has most recently been published in *River Poet's Journal* and *Stone Mountain Review*. She draws inspiration from teaching, loving and living. She would like to thank her family, the Anthologists and Robert Brewer for their support and encouragement to continue writing. A collection of her poems can be found on her blog. http://ksquaredpoetry.wordpress.com/
Kim King's Strand:
If the jaundiced sun punches a hole in the parchment sky, I must pen those words or expire.

Laurie Kolp

Laurie Kolp has a Bachelor of Science degree in Curriculum and Instruction from Texas A&M University. Laurie's recent publications include The Dead Mule's School Society of Southern Literature, poetsesspresso, Skive Magazine, The Christian Communicator, pay attention: a river of stones, Christmas Miracles and Chicken Soup for the Soul: Devotional for Troubled Times and numerous online venues. Laurie is a bimonthly contributor to Imaginary Garden with Real Toads. She has two active poetry sites: http://lkharris-kolp.blogspot.com/ and http://lkkolp.wordpress.com/.
Laurie Kolp 's Strand:
Poetry is love pouring out of my heart in metaphors and images giving life to spiritual afflatus.

Andrew Kreider

Andrew Kreider is a poet and musician based in Elkhart, Indiana. Born and raised in London, England, he moved to the United States two decades ago. His career path has included work as a stock control assistant, coat hanger factory employee, barn painter, admissions counselor, financial aid director, restaurant shift manager and pastor. Variously described as charismatic, profound, lyrical, and quirky, his work in music and poetry takes delight in throwing a sidelong glance at ordinary life. http://thepenguinpoet.blogspot.com
Andrew Kreider 's Strand:
writing like breathing, breathing for living

Catherine Lee

Catherine Lee spent her formative years in Virginia, then expatriated to a foreign country known as Texas where she currently lives with her husband and two kids. She is a student at Texas A&M University and began writing poetry in 2010 when she enrolled in a poetry class. Her work has appeared in the Blinn Literary Journal, Wilderness House Literary Journal, and a forthcoming anthology by Telling Our Stores Press (Winter 2011). She is also an International Merit Award Winner in Atlanta Review's 2011 International Poetry Competition. More of her poetry can be found at oneinchtall.com.

Catherine Lee's Strand:
I bend with ink-stained hands to gather words beneath the surface.

Amy Barlow Liberatore

Amy Barlow Liberatore blogs poetry under the name Sharp Little Pencil. As a singer/songwriter, she has worked from coast to coast in the States, as well as Bermuda and Puerto Rico. These days, music has taken a back seat to poetry; she has been published in The Awakenings Review and Thoughts That Breathe: An Anthology of Poets United, as well as online at melisma and The Pink Chameleon. She lives in Madison, WI and can be found at http://sharplittlepencil.wordpress.com/.

Amy Barlow Liberatore 's Strand:
Wherever my mind wanders, my best chance is to catch up with it

Shannon Bo Lockard

Shannon Bo Lockard is a wife and a mother, an educator, a sister, a friend, and a writer at heart, yearning for paper and pen. She writes poetry and prose that portrays her self-reflections, desires, imagination, and fears. But, she is a mother first; devotion unfading. Watching as her four children grow and change into magical people with beauty and grace is her favorite pass-time.
More of her poetry can be found at
http://www.shannonlockard.blogspot.com

Shannon Bo Lockard's S*trand:*
a smile, a tear, a stifling fear

mike Maher.
mike Maher. is the editor of Sea Giraffe Magazine, and he currently reads, writes, and edits in Philadelphia with his dog, Young Money. His poetry, fiction, and personal essays have appeared in several publications, including Contemporary American Voices, The Smoking Poet, Paper Darts, Hippocampus Magazine, The Subterranean Literary Journal, and The Copperfield Review, among others. He has a BA in English from East Stroudsburg University, where he served as the Vice President and Forum Editor of The Stroud Courier, won the Jim Barniak Award for journalism two times, and won the Martha E. Martin Award for poetry, before graduating cum laude.
mike Maher.'s Strand:
"the desire to get out some of what has gotten in, to drain the overwhelming basin of being, to live a little longer through every word on paper."

Nikki Markle
A native West Virginian, Nikki Markle is currently boiling under the Texan sun with her husband & two small children. Still paying student loans for degrees in Psychology, English, History, & Ballroom Dance Instruction & Performance, she spends her days engaged in all manner of nerdy pursuits from historical clothing recreation to writing romance novels. A lover of wit, sarcasm, & observational humor, her poetry can be found on her blog at http://poeticechoesanddancingshadows.blogspot.com
Nikki Markle 's Strand:
The focus to find a little piece of peace in pinning down that bit of something that is Me.

Buddah Moskowitz
Buddah Moskowitz was raised in the shadow of the Magic Kingdom and is the Poet Laureate of the Inland Empire. He writes like the illegitimate love child of Dorothy Parker and Charles Bukowski and his current writings are housed at http://ihatepoetry.blogspot.com. He is the editor and creator of www.virtualpoetryreading.com, a website where poets phone in their poetry to share with an international audience. His latest work is available in ebook format only, entitled "I Hate Poetry 2.0: Formatted for Mobile Devices."
Buddah Moskowitz 's Strand:
I am not an artist. I am a documentarian and I am my own favorite subject.

Bruce Niedt

Bruce is a "beneficent bureaucrat" and family man from southern NJ whose poetry has appeared in numerous print and online journals, including Writer's Digest, Writers' Journal, The Lyric, Tilt-a-Whirl, Shot Glass Journal, Four and Twenty, Mad Poets Review, paper wasp (Australia) and The Wolf (UK). His awards include the ByLine Short Fiction and Poetry Prize, first prize for poetry at the Philadelphia Writers Conference, and a Pushcart Prize nomination. He has recently had the good fortune to attend workshops led by poets Jane Hirshfield, Stephen Dunn, and Molly Peacock. His latest chapbook is Breathing Out, from Finishing Line Press. Bruce's occasional blog, "Orangepeel", can be found at http://bniedt.blogspot.com".

Bruce Niedt 's Strand:
Here are some words; here is a road. Create your journey.

Connie Peters

Connie Peters, originally from western Pennsylvania, now lives in Southwest Colorado with her husband, son, and two adults with developmental disabilities. Her daughter, also a poet, lives in Louisiana. A novelist, children's and devotional writer, and poet, Connie's work has appeared in many publications including Focus on the Family's Thriving Child, Christian Communicator, and Cup of Comfort and Heavenly Humor books. She writes regularly for The Pagosa Sun, Presidential Prayer Team and Adam Colwell's WriteWorks. She enjoys playing Canasta and Scrabble, and traveling. She has visited all of the continental United States, and has been writing a poem a day since 2004. You can read samples of her work at enthusiasticsoul.blogspot.com.

Connie Peters' Strand:
I like wrapping my feelings into little word packages, so when others open them, they laugh, cry, and experience life.

Nancy Posey

Nancy Posey lives in Hickory, North Carolina, and has been teaching English for more than twenty years, first in high school, then the last five years at the community college, a job she loves. She is a born-again poet, a fledgling mandolin student, a voracious reader, a freelance writer, and blogger. (http://discriminatingreader.com) Her poems have appeared in The Dead Mule School of Southern Literature, Wild Goose Poetry Review, Branches, and Referential Magazine. Her first chapbook Let the Lady Speak was published by Highland Creek Press after winning the Poetic Asides November 2009 Chapbook Challenge.

Nancy Posey 's Strand:
Sometimes at night, I waken, not from the sound of a rattle of someone trying the door or tree branches tapping against the window or soft footfalls outside my door, but the muse, whispering lines in my ear, prodding me to reach for a pen and paper, to capture them before they too slip back outside.

Pearl Ketover Prilik

Pearl Ketover Prilik, was raised by two people too young to tell her not to dream.

As a result she hasn't yet awakened to accept the non-poetic containment of thought, that some define as "realistic." After all sorts of personal and professional experiences she has concluded that life itself *is* a vivid dream of integrated reality and narrative. In third grade, a blue-haired straight backed teacher impressed the term "picture words" upon her which seemed to precisely articulate the way she viewed the world then and now. A list of graduate degrees, several nonfiction books published, a doctoral dissertation, an editorship of a professional psychoanalytic society newsletter, the joy of birthing one and raising three children to adulthood, while certainly holding profound personal value, informs her love for, and writing of poetry, yet does not speak directly to the road leading to *Prompted.* Stepping online several years ago, PKP found a world of "picture-word-people" at Robert Lee Brewer's blog, Poetic Asides. She became a daily contributor at PA, reaching out as time went on to other online sites (i.e. Poets United and the delightful Sunday Whirl). She now has a few hundred poems and micro-short stories on her own blog, more than a few of which have been published online, and a completed novel based on her series of "Kaitlin" poems which has been submitted and received its first beautiful rejection from a major NYC publishing house. Dr. Pearl Ketover Prilik maintains a private practice as a psychoanalyst, and continues to write on a daily basis, planning on submitting her slowly reconstituting forest of unsubmitted manuscripts, before they are someday submitted for her posthumously; more than likely by her unwavering supporter, son, Joshua Ketover. She is delighted to be part of this "cooperative collective" of poets who have slipped their virtual bonds to become kindred spirits in the dream that continues. PKP lives on the South shore of Long Island with her best friend/husband DJ. An aspect of her will always linger in the USVI, forever twenty-three, dancing barefoot on the sunlit shore of the turquoise sea with a baby on her hip. She and her work can be found at her site "Imagine" http://drpkp.com

Pearl Ketover Prilik 's *Strand:*

An infant eyelash on a newborn cheek , cinders of people dust and all between.

Jane Shlensky

Jane Shlensky has written mostly prose since earning her MFA at UNC-Greensboro, but has returned to writing poetry with the 2011 April PAD challenge at Writer's Digest. For thirty-eight years, she has taught English at high schools, universities, and community colleges in the US and China, serving as a board member and president of the North Carolina English Teachers Association, and being awarded the North Carolina Outstanding English Teacher award. Her teaching Asian Studies catalyzed her travel throughout Asia and elsewhere on Fulbrights and other study grants and resulted in a growing collection of oddities in art and literature gathered from her excursions, one of whom is her husband, Vladimir. In her spare time, she bakes, makes music, gardens, and reads too many books. Her older poetry was published in The North Carolina English Teacher, The Blue Mirror, The Crucible, and other literary magazines, but since April, she has been published by The Dead Mule School of Southern Literature, Bay Leaves, and Writer's Digest (in February, 2012).

Jane Shlensky 's Strand:

Writing requires at least as much attention as a person would devote to a friendship. If I ignore them for too long, words won't come when I call them. Due diligence and faithfulness to my own truth keep me observing, writing, and monitoring the undercurrents of my life where real discovery is made possible.

Jay Sizemore

Jay Sizemore has never lived by the sea. He has never sat in a dusty attic clickity clacking away while the ghosts of his ancestors whispered the secrets of existence in his ears. He writes poems because he has thoughts that beg solidarity, and he hopes the effort of creation strikes as true as the chisel in his gravestone, though he knows his voice blends like the blurred wings of the moth into the silence of the night. He lives in Nashville, TN, with his wife Elizabeth. They have three cats.

All his words can be read here : www.sizemorepoetry.blogspot.com

Jay Sizemore 's Strand:

words pour from wounds that eyes can't see, a blood soaking into pages, like a poultice drawing out a poison from the broken heart of beauty unseen.

a.m.trumble

Newly married, and a recent graduate a.m. is feeling like a race horse right out of the gate. She considers herself a poet mostly, but has been known on occasion to write satirical plays and spout off her quirky point of view and irreverent humor. At the moment she is heading up her group identity found, a pursuit for identity through writing at writing our way home. She also assists in the development of Poets United a blog for poets. You can find her poetry, as well as other writings (if you look around) at her blog Originals. She is also a featured spoken word poet at Buddah Moskowitz's Virtual Poetry Reading and Buddah Moskowitz's Virtual Poetry Reading 2.0 and is published at the River and a handful of stones. http://www.bttrflyscar.blogspot.com/

a.m.trumble's Strand:
a click and a spark that will push this rolling stone, which moves a bit faster with moss overgrown.

Sara Vinas

A native Californian transplanted to Florida. A worshipper of sun, sea and serendipity. She is also an artist whose inspiration for painting, drawing and poetry comes from the delight of nature. Sara has been published in trade journals and the children's poetry magazine Whimsy. She is currently working on a women's fiction manuscript of life as a gringa. Sara is eternally thankful to Robert Brewer and all the Poem A Day participants for leading her back into the joy of writing poetry and creating a community that bears all things, believes all things, hopes all things and endures all things.

Sara Vinas' Strand:
Bobbing in a sea of too much to do when I found you

Paula Wanken

Paula Wanken has a BA in secondary education, has worked as an administrative assistant for more than twenty years, and an "accidental poet" for less than one. After some encouragement by a friend to start writing, in December 2010, her blog "echoes from the silence" was born (http://whenwordsescape.wordpress.com). It wasn't long before she found her words being crafted into poetry, and once National Poetry Writing Month (NaPoWriMo) and Poetic Aside's Poem-A-Day Challenge came along, the online prompts had her hooked. Paula is grateful for the push that got her started writing, and for the online community of poets who have encouraged her to keep going.

Paula Wanken's Strand:
words become pictures and pictures become poems

Claudette J. Young

Claudette J. Young did her undergrad and graduate work at Ball State University in Sociology, Psychology, and Gerontology. She has taught at both the elementary and college level. She began writing in 2008 and has had poetry published in one anthology, as well as in the on-line magazines Soft Whispers, The River Journal, and a few others. She also has numerous children's stories and non-fiction pieces published both in print and on-line. She considers herself to be an eclectic writer and enjoys that position.

Claudette J. Young's Strand:
A whisperer electrifies my brain

A note from the editor:

Remember

Recall and hold fast to all
that flushed your face and
quickened your heart
that had you pause in
awestruck wonderment
that had you throw off your shoes
and dance in bare feet - even once
on the sandy shores
of receding time

pkp

Appendix:

The following are the ten chosen prompts, reproduced with permission from Writer's Digest and Robert Lee Brewer as they originally appeared on the blog Poetic Asides by Robert Lee Brewer.

1. Time of day [April 9, 2011]
For today's prompt, write a time of day poem. In fact, make the title of your poem the time of day. For instance, "5:54 a.m.," "2:23 p.m.," "Midnight," etc. Then, write your poem. Of course, different things happen at different times of day. So have fun with it.

2. Inverted Pyramid Poem [July 22, 2010]
Pack all the essential information in the first stanza, slightly less important information in the second stanza, even less important information in the third, etc. The idea is that an editor would be able to cut the bottom of the piece if needed without losing any of the essential "news." Write a poem like this that gets the what, who, where, when, why and how near the top.

3. Message In a bottle [April 20, 2011]
For today's prompt, write a message in a bottle poem. Imagine that your poem is being rolled up and put in a bottle for someone to read. Or if you want to come at it in a different way, think of it as a poem left in a time capsule or hidden away in your sock drawer. By the way, I would like to thank Nancy Posey for giving me the idea for today's prompt.

4. Prayer [April 24, 2011]
For today's prompt, write a prayer poem. Your prayer poem could be religious, but it doesn't have to be. People can pray to make it to work on time. Or to be rich. Or even for the rain. It's completely up to you what you're poem is about. (I pray that everyone is respectful of each other's prayer poems today.)

5. Write a love poem and an anti-love poem [April 19, 2011]
Today is a "Two for Tuesday" prompt. In fact, it's one of my favorite prompts of each challenge. Poets can:
1. Write a love poem.
2. Write an anti-love poem.
I'm more of a love poem guy myself. The love poem doesn't have to be romantic love; there are other types. The anti-love poem can be against love or against love poems.

6. Type of Person [April 4, 2011]
For today's prompt, pick a type of person and write a poem about him or her. To help set the scene, you may want to title your poem as who the type of person is. For instance, you could write a poem titled "Firefighter," "Cynic," "Optimist," "Teacher," "2-year-old," etc. The list is endless.

7. Write a "location" poem [November 3, 2010]
For today's prompt, write a location poem. The poem can be about a location, but it doesn't have to be. It could also just incorporate a location into the poem (like a love poem in Paris or something). This poem could also state your feelings about location in general.

8. Water [April 2, 2010]
For today's prompt, write a water poem. The poem could be specifically about water or just include water somewhere within the poem. You could even write about water-based phenomenon, such as rainbows or water spouts.

9. All I want [April 17, 2009]
For today's prompt, I want you to write a poem with the following title: "All I want is (blank)," where you fill in the blank with a word or phrase of your choosing. Some example titles, then, could be: "All I want is to eat fried chicken"; "All I want is world peace"; "All I want is for everyone to tell me I'm beautiful"; or "All I want is a handful of quarters."

10. After leaving here [April 30, 2011]
For today's prompt, write an "after leaving here" poem. This poem could be about leaving an actual place, a relationship, or even this challenge. We leave many places and things every day without much ado, including rooms, vehicles, people (both those we know and complete strangers), etc. And to make this poem even more interesting is that there is presumably something that will be done after the leaving, whether that's something fun, sad, hopeful, or whatever.

www.ingramcontent.com/pod-product-compliance
Lightning Source LLC
Chambersburg PA
CBHW031547040426
42452CB00006B/221